Succeeding on Your
Primary PGCE

Education at SAGE

SAGE is a leading international publisher of journals, books, and electronic media for academic, educational, and professional markets.

Our education publishing includes:

- accessible and comprehensive texts for aspiring education professionals and practitioners looking to further their careers through continuing professional development

- inspirational advice and guidance for the classroom

- authoritative state of the art reference from the leading authors in the field

Find out more at: **www.sagepub.co.uk/education**

Succeeding on Your Primary PGCE

Graham Birrell,
Helen Taylor and
Hellen Ward

SAGE

Los Angeles | London | New Delhi
Singapore | Washington DC

SAGE Publications Ltd
1 Oliver's Yard
55 City Road
London EC1Y 1SP

SAGE Publications Inc.
2455 Teller Road
Thousand Oaks, California 91320

SAGE Publications India Pvt Ltd
B 1/I 1 Mohan Cooperative Industrial Area
Mathura Road
New Delhi 110 044

SAGE Publications Asia-Pacific Pte Ltd
33 Pekin Street #02-01
Far East Square
Singapore 048763

Library of Congress Control Number: 2009938707

British Library Cataloguing in Publication data

A catalogue record for this book is available from
the British Library

ISBN 978-1-84920-029-5
ISBN 978-1-84920-030-1 (pbk)

Typeset by C&M Digitals (P) Ltd, Chennai, India
Printed by MPG Books Group, Bodmin, Cornwall
Printed on paper from sustainable resources

Mixed Sources
Product group from well-managed
forests and other controlled sources
www.fsc.org Cert no. SA-COC-1565
© 1996 Forest Stewardship Council
FSC

Contents

Acknowledgements   vii
About the authors   viii

1   So you want to be a primary teacher?   1
Graham Birrell

2   Making the most of your time before the course begins   9
Graham Birrell

3   Making the most of your time in school: preparation
and organisation   20
Helen Taylor

4   Making the most of your time in school: learning
and teaching   32
Helen Taylor

5   Being academic   44
Hellen Ward

6   Being positive   60
Graham Birrell

7   Being reflective   71
William Stow

8   Getting a job   85
Hellen Ward

9   Succeeding on your induction   99
Helen Taylor

Appendix: Getting on a primary PGCE   111
  Hellen Ward

Glossary   116
Useful websites   119
References   121
Index   122

Acknowledgements

We would like to thank the many PGCE students we have worked with over the years. These students have inspired us to write this book and have given us invaluable feedback to help us to understand the issues they face in being successful on their PGCE. Particular thanks must go to those students who have provided case study material. Thanks are also due to the colleagues we have worked with, who have regularly discussed experiences, ideas and issues with us.

Another important group of people to mention are the headteachers, mentors and other teachers who have supported our students in primary schools, in Kent, Medway and Sussex. These teachers have shared their delights and frustrations about supporting our students and helped us to identify the issues that schools face in their mentoring work.

We would also like to acknowledge the help we have received in the writing process, especially with proof reading and editing. These willing readers and able critics have included Jack Dhainaut, Shirley Taylor, Caroline Hawker and Keith Remnant.

Also thank you to Dan Port, Kerry Crane, Maurice George, Charlotte Ward, Carolyn Weston, Sandra Dwarte, Hester Mackay and David Simon without whom key content in this book would not have been possible.

Jude Bowen, our commissioning editor, has been particularly encouraging and positive throughout the writing project; this has made us feel that the book is worthwhile. Thank you, Jude.

About the authors

Graham Birrell For many years, Graham has been the Programme Director of the PGCE (Primary) Full-time at Canterbury Christ Church University. As well as running the PGCE he is responsible for the teaching of primary history at the university. Prior to this he was a teacher in two primary schools in Kent.

Helen Taylor Helen is the Programme Director for the PGCE Primary Part-time at Canterbury Christ Church University. Her work also involves teaching primary mathematics to student teachers and mentor training for experienced teachers supporting students during their professional placements. She taught across the age range in primary schools in Kent and was a deputy headteacher.

Hellen Ward Hellen is Programme Director for Modular PGCE Primary and Secondary at Canterbury Christ Church University. As well as teaching primary science at the university, she is also an independent education consultant actively involved with teachers in a number of Local Authorities. Hellen has written several books and a number of other publications, and has developed teaching resources and teaching materials to support the teaching and learning of science.

Contributor

William Stow William has been working as a tutor in primary education at Canterbury Christ Church University for 14 years and is currently the Head of Postgraduate Teacher Training at the University and was formerly Programme Director of the Modular PGCE. His teaching during this time has been focused mainly on primary history and professional studies. William's research interests centre on PGCE student teachers' reflections on their professional development.

1

So you want to be a primary teacher?

Graham Birrell

this chapter

- will help you to make up your mind, if you are considering teaching as a career;
- provides information on the different sorts of routes into teaching.

Why read this book?

This book is not aimed at telling you how to be a great teacher. It isn't a textbook for a PGCE; its aim is not to provide a 'how to guide'; we don't want to supply rigorous academic support for your university assignments or how to get through the teaching placements when you're in school. Instead, what this book is about is offering some insight, guidance and helpful advice on how you might wish to approach a PGCE and all its component parts. It wants to share with you some of the collective experience of PGCE course directors and what we believe makes a successful PGCE student.

Between us, we have decades of experience on teaching and leading PGCEs and in that time we have spent many hours discussing successful PGCE students. During this we have learned a lot from these students, about how they have approached the course and about exactly why they have done so well. After many years of talking to our students and to each other we thought it might be useful to share our experiences with you. This book puts together basic principles and advice in one place, to give you a head start on successfully completing your PGCE.

PGCEs can be a struggle or they can be a liberating, fulfilling and mind-stretching exercise in personal and professional development. After over 20 years of collective experience of teaching on and leading PGCE programmes, we believe we can help you to achieve the latter rather than simply the former. This book has been structured and written to help you in achieving the very most from your PGCE year (and hopefully beyond). There are chapters on key areas of the year, from successfully completing university elements, to thriving in school and even to landing that crucial first job, and this book aims to support you through what is likely to be the most (or one of the most) challenging professional years of your life.

As stated previously, this book is very much *not* meant to be a 'how-to' guide or a step-by-step walk through. We believe in individualised routes through the course, and such a book would suggest there are simple answers to complex questions that everyone can tick off in the same way. There is also no quick-fix to the PGCE and the answers to the questions you'll face on the course are far more likely to come from within rather than from a manual.

What this book hopes to achieve, based on our experience of successfully overseeing literally thousands of teaching students, is a *philosophy* towards being successful on a primary PGCE. Not a 'how to do it' but a 'how to approach it'. After working with so many students for so long, the differences between those who do well and those who struggle can be quite clear. Students who have that liberating, fulfilling and mind-stretching experience commonly approach the course in very different ways to those who don't. We want to share that approach with you, so that you too can have that experience and become better teachers of our children as a result.

Are you sure you want to be a teacher?

Teaching really isn't for everyone and for many some stories that regularly do the rounds, either in the press or amongst friends and families, would be more than enough to prevent them applying. A perception amongst many is that it is all about long hours spent planning, preparing and marking, constant stress, difficult parents, relentless new initiatives from the government, the seemingly ever increasing concerns over poorly behaved children, Ofsted inspections, SATs and league tables, etc., etc. On top of all this, teaching as a career choice has a somewhat mixed reputation. Teachers themselves have long sought the same kind of status as lawyers and doctors, but the reality is that they are only very rarely talked of in the same breath.

This is especially true of primary school teachers, where there is a very flawed perception that you don't have to be particularly bright or intellectual to succeed in the job. After all, just exactly how hard is it to make stuff out of junk and write pretty little stories about fairies and what you did in the holidays? Part of this image comes from the fact that the normal primary school set-up involves no subject specialist teaching, so therefore the theory goes that those with an in-depth understanding of subjects would be more likely to end up teaching in secondary schools. This understanding of primary teaching as not being particularly academic is neither helpful nor true, but can be found even in the most surprising of quarters. Rather ironically for someone co-authoring a book about succeeding on a Primary PGCE, I actually began my journey into teaching wanting to be a secondary school teacher (for similar reasons to those discussed above, e.g. I wanted to inspire 'academic excellence' in my subject – history) so I applied and was accepted onto a Secondary PGCE. As part of this I had to gain some observation experience at a primary school before the course began. Much to my surprise I discovered that I really enjoyed it, and after a few weeks of my secondary course realised that I much preferred working with younger children. Fortunately, I was able to transfer onto the Primary PGCE and when I saw my secondary tutor for the final time his straight-faced parting words were 'I hope you have a nice time with the plasticine'.

All this isn't to say that primary teachers aren't respected in society, but the perception of many is all too often shaped by the regularly negative stories on it in the media. For example, how did people react when you told them you were thinking of becoming a primary teacher? Was there overwhelming delight and pride? Or was there something of a reserved, cautious reaction followed by the words that began this section: 'Are you sure?'

In truth, if you've had this reaction to what is, in your opinion, exciting news, don't be disappointed. In fact, I'd say it was about right. Teaching, and since it's the subject of this book, primary school teaching, is *not* something to enter into lightly. You do have to be sure: very, very sure. You need to know what you're letting yourself in for, and if you don't that makes you a little foolish and naïve.

Now if this all sounds a somewhat negative then don't worry, because there is of course another side to this story. Teaching can be a fabulously rewarding, life-long career. Days are filled with variety, unexpected events, hilarity, challenge and, when done well, you really do regularly get those moments when you realise you have made a positive (and even life-changing) difference to the lives of other people. Yes, it is hard work, but there are few jobs where you can say with hand on heart you are capable of potentially making such an incredibly positive effect on so many people's lives.

So how do you know you're sure?

A large number of people who apply to train to be a teacher have a slightly misty-eyed impression of what primary school teaching is all about. You can see this in their applications, in their interview and, if they get that far, in their first few weeks on the course. This can be observed in the statement 'I want to be primary school teacher because I really like children'.

Now, we're not saying that liking children isn't important, or even more ridiculously that it's actually more important to not like children. The point is that 'liking children' is very far from the best reason for wanting to be a teacher. 'Liking children' is really not going to get you very far in actually 'teaching' children anything. Rather unsurprisingly, it's not going to hurt, but children don't automatically learn or want to learn simply because their teacher likes them.

Very few experienced teachers will say they enjoy teaching because they 'like children'. The more experience you gain, the more you will come to appreciate the pleasure in 'working with children' (which is subtly, but importantly different to 'teaching children') and in inspiring children and facilitating learning and developing enquiring, inquisitive, critical and challenging minds.

If you haven't done so already, there is really only one way to properly answer the question 'Why do you want to be a teacher?' and that is to go and spend some time in a primary school, and a state primary school at that. This is not to make a statement about the independent sector, but the practical aim of Primary PGCEs is about meeting the government standards for Qualified Teacher Status (QTS) in the state sector. A very practical point of also gaining this experience is that without it, it's unlikely you're going to get a PGCE place anyway.

 reflective task

If you haven't done so already, you will need to get some experience in a primary school. To help you decide if teaching is for you, think carefully about the following questions:

- Did you get a realistic flavour of what the job involved?

- Did you ask the teachers in the school(s) about what their jobs entailed?

- Did the teachers seem to enjoy what they did? If not, why not?

- Did you enjoy it?
- Did the children respond positively to you?
- Could you explain things (fairly) clearly to them?
- Can you see skills and attributes in yourself that would be transferable to the classroom?

If you answered 'yes' to most, if not all of these questions, then you're making a far more informed decision about becoming a teacher, certainly far more informed than 'I like children'. In fact, many people reading this book may have already applied and been offered a place on a Primary PGCE, or even started one, and if so deserve a well done on a great decision. If you answered 'no' to most of the questions then that might be telling you something!

What courses could you apply for?

Although there are many different types of course available (e.g. full-time routes, part-times routes, modular routes, etc.), for postgraduates interested in the primary age phase, there are essentially three main ways you can qualify: the PGCE (Professional Graduate Certificate in Education – or Postgraduate Certificate if you attain more than 40 credits towards a Master's degree as part of the course), and in Scotland the PGDE (the Professional Graduate Diploma in Education), which is essentially the same course as a PGCE; the Graduate Teacher Programme (GTP); or School Centred Initial Teacher Training (SCITT).

PGCEs, whether full-time, part-time or modular, will all involve significant periods of time at a Higher Education institution, usually a university, where participants will attend large numbers of lectures and seminars on courses looking at the themes, issues and subjects in primary teaching. These courses will be assessed through things like assignments, oral presentations, poster presentations, etc. Most universities now assess some or all of the university course assessment at Master's level, enabling successful students to gain part of a Master's whilst on the PGCE. As well as attendance at university, all PGCEs will involve two, three, or maybe even four placements in at least two different schools. These placements (and especially the last one, which is normally the longest and most strenuous in terms of expectations) must be passed in order to achieve Qualified Teacher Status (QTS).

The GTP is significantly different to a PGCE in that in the first instance those participating are not technically students, as they are employed by a school and must undertake the majority of their training full-time in that school. Participants (or trainees as they are commonly known) will usually attend some sessions in a partnership setting, often a neighbouring university or Local Authority, and those partners will be heavily involved in an assessment of the course, which will involve demonstrating an achievement of the Standards for QTS overwhelmingly throughout the time (and this predominantly means teaching time) spent in the employing school. GTP students will also attend a second school for a short assessed period.

SCITTs are provided by groups of local schools, again, often in partnership with a university or college. There is a wide variety of SCITTs and so if you are interested you would need to spend some time investigating their differences, but typically they are somewhere in between a PGCE and GTP in that you spend more time in school than on a PGCE, but you would attend more taught sessions on primary teaching theory and practice than on a GTP. Many SCITTs will also involve an assessment of coursework (e.g. essays) as well as an assessment of teaching. In return, on a successful completion, many SCITTs will also award a PGCE as well as QTS.

So why choose a PGCE?

As you'd expect from a book about succeeding on a Primary PGCE written by three course directors of Primary PGCEs, we're obviously going to be pretty positive about choosing this route into teaching. This is certainly not to denigrate GTP or SCITT routes, which are ideal for many, but we believe PGCEs offer an excellent route into teaching through the opportunity not only to spend significant periods in seminar discussions on the key educational theories that underpin successful teaching and learning, but also to spend extended time in schools to put those theories to the test in the classroom.

At this point you may be asking yourself whether you would feel comfortable with the theoretical components of a PGCE, especially as teaching is of course a highly practical profession. You may also have come across some teachers who were quite dismissive of the more theoretical aspects of the teacher education course and who said they had little time to think about theory during a typical school day because they were so busy getting on with actually being with the children and doing things like lesson preparation, meeting parents and organising trips. However, as Primary PGCE course directors we passionately believe that teaching is enormously influenced by theoretical perspectives. A simple way to think about this is to consider how ridiculous it would be to argue that there is only one accepted theory of how people learn. Simply appreciating that this is not a well-founded argument opens up the possibility of learning and appreciating alternative beliefs about how people acquire knowledge, skills, attitudes, concepts and understanding.

Furthermore, walk into any staffroom on any day and you will hear theoretical conversations taking place, perhaps without teachers even realising it, for example, when Reception teachers question whether it is right that some of their youngest children should be in formal schooling already, or when teachers with very challenging children ask whether they should be in a special school setting rather than a mainstream setting. All these issues, and many, many more, are theoretical and most have had enormous amounts of research already (or continuously being) written about them.

Although PGCEs are typically less than a year in length, we believe that this still gives you time to reflect on and learn about some key education research. Any successful nation needs an informed and educated teaching profession; teachers ignorant of an understanding of their trade are unlikely to be able to help their pupils achieve their full potential, or to be able to offer an informed and professional viewpoint when the profession's integrity is challenged.

We see PGCE courses as providing a tremendous opportunity to learn about the theory behind teaching, and through the school placements to apply those theories in the classroom. Chapter 5 in this book will talk about this in more depth.

Significantly however, and Chapter 7 will go into this in far more detail, in common with all the educational research conducted on what makes a successful teacher, we believe that reflection is a crucial, perhaps the *most* crucial, tool in a teacher's armoury. Teachers or student teachers need time and space (or need to make the time and space) to sit back and analyse why a lesson went so well or conversely why a lesson descended into chaos. Again, we believe that PGCEs can give you that time, and powerfully, especially as a great deal of research suggests that learning is a collaborative and social experience, that they provide opportunities for this reflection to be undertaken both with experienced tutors and with peers in the same situation.

Making good choices

You may be thinking about applying for a PGCE or you may be about to start one. You may even be a student on one already. If you are making an informed decision based on your experienced knowledge of teaching and of yourself, all of these would be good choices. We hope that in any of these cases you will find this a useful and helpful book.

7

Although we passionately believe in the value of a PGCE, we know such an achievement is not easy. Not only is it very hard work and involves a great deal of commitment in terms and time and effort, but it also needs a commitment in terms of thinking and learning about thinking and learning. This book cannot make the course easy, but it might make it easier. Reading it can't guarantee you'll enjoy the course, but it might make it more enjoyable. Most importantly though, whilst this book can't make you a good teacher, it might make you a better one.

2

Making the most of your time before the course begins

Graham Birrell

this chapter

- provides some constructive ideas as to why and how you should prepare for your PGCE;
- will help you develop a personal philosophy towards teaching.

Like all challenges, PGCEs shouldn't be entered into lightly and without forethought or preparation. Mentally, you need to get in the right place, but intellectually and academically you also need to get ready. This chapter does exactly what it promises and although it's most likely to be useful to you if you have already been accepted onto a PGCE, even if you're still only at the 'thinking about it' stage I'm sure that you will find it helpful, as it will give you an excellent idea of what's involved before the course even starts. Hopefully, you'll find it's full of useful advice and ideas to make the absolute most of the period before you start your PGCE, so that when the course begins you aren't just ready, but are actually one step ahead.

Developing your understanding and philosophy

I've talked to quite a few programme directors of Primary PGCEs and experience in school is the thing they cite as the most important factor in firstly getting on a PGCE, and then being prepared for both the course and for life as a teacher. This of course makes complete sense, as how else can you tell if you will enjoy school life or if you have the skills and attributes required? For those simple reasons, almost all primary PGCEs will stipulate school experience as an entry requirement. Furthermore, once accepted, most primary PGCEs will demand a further observation period in schools before the course starts.

However, think very carefully about how to get the absolute best out of your observation experience, as not all students use this wisely. Universities that have a one or two week pre-course observation 'placement' built in to their PGCE will almost certainly send you a guidance pack, full of activities you could undertake, and my advice is to follow this closely as it will have been put together by people who really know what they're talking about after having lived and breathed primary education for a very long time. Later on in this chapter are some examples of the sort of activities you should undertake when observing; but more than just structured tasks, you should use this time to think very carefully about your *philosophy* of teaching.

  reflective task – philosophy

1. As honestly as you can, on a piece of paper right down your top five priorities as a teacher. What will be important to you when you are teaching? What will be the signs that you are doing a good job?

2. Now put them in order with the one that is most important to you at the top.

3. Study these carefully; what do you think they tell you about what you value most in teaching?

For example, did you include a well behaved class on your list? If so, how high up the list was it? What about pupil learning? Was that higher than good behaviour? If not, do you value good behaviour more than learning? Or do you think the latter can only be achieved after the former has been established?

What sort of learning do you value? Do you think that children should learn lots of subject knowledge or more skills, concepts and attitudes? For example, and this is an area hotly contested by people interested in history in schools, should children learn all about the key events in the reign of Henry VIII or that there are different interpretations of the merits (or lack of them) of Henry as a king?

Before people start PGCEs, many of them will have a fairly clear idea of what sort of teacher they want to be. In the early days of teaching, many new students will see simply controlling the class as a clear measure of success. This is perfectly understandable, but the obvious next question is just *how important* is it? For some it will quickly become secondary to other factors, such as pupil enjoyment or empowerment, but for others it will continue to be central to their thinking. Many students' ideas of what 'good teaching' actually is stem from their own experiences of teaching, with these either running in parallel or in complete contrast. For example, students from fairly traditional educational backgrounds will often believe strongly in traditional approaches to teaching, or in contrast will strongly question them.

Relating back to the reflective task, some teachers you will observe will take a very overt controlling grip on their class, insisting on silence or near silence, the 'working hum', while their class works. Other teachers will have what appears to be seething, teeming chaos going on, which despite what it looks like seems to work for them. Some teachers will believe firmly in closely directed tasks with pretty much fixed outcomes and expectations (e.g. children *will* walk out knowing x and y), while others will believe in child-directed, independent activities with a more risk-taking approach where outcomes aren't fixed in advance (e.g. children *may* walk out knowing x and y, but *possibly* also z too).

You will doubtless have your own views on the approach you feel is best, and speaking personally I believe it is better to have some idea of what sort of teacher you want to be and to be passionate about it, rather than have no idea at all and be rather apathetic. I would definitely challenge you at least to think about what sort of teacher you aim to become, and you can use your observation in school to begin to form an opinion.

However, it's also important to be *open-minded*. Don't be so blinded by your own beliefs about what 'good teaching' is that you aren't prepared to consider alternative strategies. This is where observation is so crucial. Experience in the classroom is simply vital not only in learning some fantastic tips and ideas, such as how to get children changed for PE with the minimum amount of fuss (and this remains one of the biggest challenges for any primary teacher, especially those in the early years!), but also in terms of observing some of the many different styles and approaches that you will come across in primary classrooms.

For this reason, try and observe as many teachers as you possibly can, with as many different age ranges as you possibly can, in as many schools as you can.

You may or may not be surprised to learn that primary schools can have very different ethoses, perspectives and priorities. Sometimes you can learn a lot about these simply by walking through the front door. University tutors become fairly adept at judging this from visiting their students in many different sorts of schools whilst on school placement. However, even the inexperienced can learn things quickly, so just be willing to look about you and take things in.

For example, one school I heard of recently (Claxton, 2009) had a display in the foyer of one class's attempt at making rockets. They were fairly tatty, not particularly good rockets and clearly weren't likely to be very effective in taking their payloads into orbit. Not such a good first impression then? Well, actually no, because on closer inspection, next to each rocket was an analysis from each pupil as to where they had gone wrong and how they had corrected their errors when making the final and finished product. These were simply prototypes, and if you wanted to see the final thing you were directed to their classroom. This told you a great deal about their teacher (and the school's validation of his or her teaching by having this display as the first thing that all new visitors to the school saw), who valued the process as much as the outcome, who considered errors and mistakes were to be celebrated and learnt from, and who showed how effective design comes from planning and persistence.

Clearly the physical environment is important and not just in terms of attractive displays; for example, how are the tables and chairs arranged? Rows suggest the teacher prefers a more traditional approach, groups suggest a more discussion-led style. However, what is perhaps more important than the physical environment is the emotional environment. How are the children spoken to? Are their contributions valued? What is the reaction to their errors? Do they seem at ease in each other's and the adults' company? All these things can range from school to school.

Look closely at some of the more mundane elements of the school. For example, how the children are shepherded around the school can be interesting. Most schools will require high standards of order from their pupils at times like coming in from the playground or going into assembly. These can resemble a military parade ground affair of perfect lines of children filing in and out of halls and classrooms. Other schools will have a more laissez-faire approach; for example, I know of some where lining up has been banned and where the children are allowed to come into the hall for assembly and sit wherever they like, just like adults would. What do these different practices tell you about such schools? What do they believe is important? Is there evidence from elsewhere as to their values and principles?

You can learn a great deal about teaching from simply observing the day-to-day operation of a school. As Helen Taylor observes in Chapter 4, even to this day, every time I go into a new school I learn something about teaching and about schools. I regularly challenge my own beliefs and question assumptions. To give one small, but hopefully interesting, example, I go to Germany every year to visit students who are on a student teacher exchange programme. One of the immediate things I noticed the first time I went was that at break-times in every school I visited, the children behaved in the corridors exactly the same as they would do in the playground; so you can imagine this was chaos, and when the bell went they simply ambled back into their various classes without being told or directed, a class at a time as you would see in the overwhelming majority of British primary schools.

At first I couldn't believe they were allowed to do this, and the teachers didn't seem to mind as they wandered through the mayhem between staff-room and classroom. However, what happened next in each school was fascinating. Not only did the children calm right down immediately upon coming back into class, but they were also incredibly attentive and engaged at the start of the lesson, appearing to be almost different children entirely. This made me question whether our insistence on order and lining up was important or even perhaps counter-productive.

Now, we shouldn't generalise from only a small number of classes and especially when there may have been myriad cultural and educational factors that were hidden and unknown to me, but it nonetheless challenged my perceptions on one very minor aspect of 'effective teaching' and whether the norm in this country's schools was really effective. I would similarly challenge you to use your observation time to confront your own beliefs on what successful schools and teachers look like.

However, as well as thinking more esoterically and theoretically about some general aspects of what you observe taking place in school, there are some very clear practical tasks you could and should engage in that will help you to gain a clearer understanding of how to be a teacher before the course even starts. As I said earlier, each university will provide some suggested tasks and you should follow these, but some examples are available below.

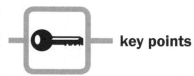 **key points**

Some suggestions for practical observation tasks

- Ask the school for a copy of the behaviour policy. Ask yourself: why was this written? What was the objective? Who wrote it? How often is it reviewed? Who is it given to? Is it followed in the school? If so, how do I think this has been achieved?
- Ask your teacher for a copy of a medium-term plan. Annotate it with your thoughts. Was it written by an individual or team? Is it purely about one subject or is it cross-curricular? How does it cater for differing abilities? How does it plan for progression, for example lessons building on each other in stages?

- Observe one child closely for 30 minutes. Devise your own way of recording the child's behaviour during that period, for example are they working or playing alone, talking to another child, interacting with the teacher, waiting, etc. Which behaviours predominated? What factors affected this? Did the teacher influence the behaviour in any way (remember that 'behaviours' can be positive as well as negative)? Try this again with a contrasting age phase. Did the behaviours differ in the two phases? If so, why?
- Identify some children who are having difficulty with a task. Then identify the nature of the difficulty. Talk to the children about it to discover their understanding. Reflect on this discussion in terms of why pupils find some tasks challenging and how they approach overcoming them.
- Observe how boys and girls behave in a lesson. Do they interact differently with children of the same and opposite gender? Do they gain the same amount of attention and interaction from the teacher? A simple tally chart could reveal some interesting results.

For more information on observation, Chapter 4 has some excellent guidance for your actual teaching placements.

Here are some words of advice from a former PGCE student, who suggests some ways to make the most of the time you have before you start the course.

 case study

Mushtaq

Mushtaq was a highly successful student teacher, something his tutors felt could in large part be attributed to his reflective approach.

'It can be tempting when you first receive the confirmation that you are enrolled on a teacher training course to do absolutely nothing. I certainly did ... for about two days, and then the panic set in! "I wasn't very good at maths at school", "I can't remember what I learnt in science", "The last time I did history I was 13!" I found that it was a good idea to write down the things that were worrying me and jot down some thoughts about where I could find help with them.

Books and the internet are great, but if I had to recommend just one thing to do before starting the course it's to talk; pick out two or three things that you really want to focus on understanding before you start your course – don't rely on picking up everything once the course has started. I wish I had made some contacts at interview day, this would have given me the opportunity to get in touch with some other trainees in the same boat.

Looking back at my preparation I think I probably should have tried to improve my subject knowledge a little more. I would recommend spending some time brushing up on the areas that you know you are weaker in before the course starts. Trying to do this once the course has started is really hard due to the demands on your time.

Whilst I enjoyed the observation placement I did not make the most of the opportunity. I think it is vital that you go in there with a clear idea of what you want to get out of it. I recommend noting maybe three things you really want to focus on, like: what's it like in a year 6 classroom?; how does the teacher deliver literacy?; even, how does the staffroom work?! Also, don't be afraid to ask things. It may take a couple of days to build up the confidence, but if you are professional and choose your time I found that most staff are more than willing to help. A proactive approach will help you arrive at your first teaching placement better prepared and ready to get stuck in.'

Do your research, be informed

One of the great myths that many people hold about training to be a teacher is that whatever sort of course you take it will be dominated by being told how to teach, learning lots of excellent tips for how to get children to do what you want, and engaging in a series of university sessions that will go through the sorts of things you could try out in schools. The fact that PGCEs aren't like this in reality comes as quite a shock to some, as does the significant emphasis on research and theory. Most sessions will involve some sort of reading beforehand of recommended books, chapters or articles and most students will learn much about teaching from this.

Give yourself a head start and engage in some reading before the course begins; your university will have their own recommended reading lists and you should follow these. Clearly this makes sense in terms of being informed about some important background reading about teaching. However, more than this, it is likely to make the start of the course, and quite possibly the rest of it too, an awful lot easier. Your tutors will make some reasonable assumptions about you in the first few sessions on the course; that you are intelligent, that you are motivated, that you are interested in working with children and that you know something about teaching already. Your sessions with these tutors will obviously go better for you if you can interact with them at a higher level of understanding and early reading will help to achieve this. Getting off to a great start is obviously what you will want.

Something that many students (and researchers) find useful is a reading journal. You can start this with your pre-course reading; as well as making notes on the things you have read, write short summaries of the key points discussed in each article/chapter and provide a précis of the main arguments. If you do this properly, you should find this invaluable both in your growing understanding of teaching and also when it comes to writing the assignments on your course.

However, there are also other sorts of research you can engage in. If you didn't already do this for your interview, find out as much as you can about your university and your course. Obviously you can visit the university's website to do this, but there are other places you can gather information from. For some fairly helpful statistical information you could visit www. unistats.com which compares different universities. For a more detailed commentary you could take a look at the recent Ofsted reports for your university's primary education courses (like schools, these are inspected).

Perhaps best of all, try to get some insider perspectives from students already on the course or from those who have already done it, or from those people, like you, who are about to start. There are loads of places on the web you can do this, ranging from independent social network sites, to the university's own social networks (often called 'nings'), to internet forums hosted by respected organisations like the TES (*Times Educational Supplement*). As well as making friends with other people who are about to start the course, you're also likely to obtain some useful information from some of your university's alumni. Be warned though; remember that the informality of social networking has very little in common with professional networking – for example some students and teachers have landed in some serious trouble for being unprofessional about schools on social network sites. Also, do approach some students' comments with a degree of caution as the forums will occasionally attract the disgruntled minority who may not tell you the full story behind any dissatisfaction!

Another area of research you should consider engaging in is improving your subject knowledge. It's likely to have been some time since you studied many of the subjects taught in primary schools, so a good place to start is to obtain the latest copy of the National Curriculum and take a look at what is covered. Undertake a needs analysis exercise to identify where you think you may have weaknesses and then get on with correcting these.

In order to obtain QTS you must also pass three skills tests in maths, English and ICT. Many on-line or high street bookshops sell guides to passing these that will also help you to analyse your strengths and weaknesses in such areas. Furthermore, the TDA website at www.tda.gov.uk has practice tests you can take that will give you even more idea of what is involved.

 case study

Kelly

Kelly was a highly positive and motivated student who always tried to see the best side of everything, something which contributed to her success on the PGCE.

'Although it is difficult to prepare for the unexpected I did select books from the recommended list, which provided helpful information about behaviour management and children's physiological processes. I also undertook the required observation period and decided to focus on planning, whether this was day-to-day planning or termly. I had previous experience in classrooms, but had never thought about how the teacher knew what to teach in every lesson. I enjoyed working through the pack provided by my university as this helped me focus on other areas such as subject knowledge, the teacher's role and the use of the Teaching Assistant (TA).

Social networking sites were also helpful as I found ex-PGCE students who clarified some of the things that could happen on the course. Some especially useful advice I was given was to begin to read children's books over the summer, and this helped me get to know the types of literature children were reading and the characters that were popular in children's culture. I also used my time to improve my maths knowledge, using revision websites and some maths practice papers. I think that if you feel weaker in one area of the curriculum then it is good to use the summer to help you strengthen this. I primarily did this so that when I started the course I could take my QTS skills tests as soon as possible.

Preparing for the course is down to personal choice. For me I enjoyed being able to look into things before the course commenced, and used the observation weeks to help understand certain aspects of teaching. Being well prepared from the start of the course also helped me to form a view of what sort of teacher I wanted to be; organised, flexible in my approach, and able to take advantage of as much information as possible.'

key points

Like all good Scouts, be prepared

- Look at the book list your university has sent you, undertake some suggested reading and start a reading journal.
- Read about your university using official and unofficial sources.
- Brush up on your subject knowledge, after analysing which areas need addressing.

Get ready

If you were thinking that the months before the course were going to be the calm before the storm, this wasn't entirely accurate. It's true that the expectations are fairly gentle, but at the same time, if you want to make the absolute most of the PGCE, you need to aim to get a head start through some effective preparation.

I obviously haven't mentioned some fairly important practical information that you will need to engage in before you start, such as sorting out your accommodation, your money (e.g. fees, loans, etc.) and filling in the copious amounts of paperwork that universities require from you (health declarations, Criminal Record Bureau checks, etc.). However, this is basically administrative legwork that has to be done. This chapter has focused on aiming to prepare you mentally for the course, and for your life in teaching. Clearly the more you can learn about teaching and your own personal attitudes and beliefs towards it, the better. The PGCE is possibly going to be one of the most, if not *the* most, intensive period of work and study in your life to date, so anything you can do in advance to help prepare you for this makes sense.

What are you waiting for? Go and get ready!

further reading

Arthur, J., Grainger, T. and Wray, D. (eds) (2006) *Learning to Teach in the Primary School*. Abingdon: Routledge. This is a good 'catch-all' introduction to primary school teaching, written by people with huge amounts of experience of teacher-training courses. It's easy to read, and a good place to start for those with little experience.

Claxton, G. (2009) *What's the Point of School? Rediscovering the Heart of Education*. London: Oneworld. A thought-provoking look at modern schools. This won't necessarily teach you a great deal about 'the basics', but with any luck it will make you think about whether modern schools work and about your part in them.

Palmer, J. (ed.) (2001) *Fifty Modern Thinkers on Education: From Piaget to the Present Day*. London: Routledge. This is a very handy beginner's guide to some key educational theorists, their philosophies, and their influence. Piaget, Vygotsky and Bruner are typically what many universities start with, so read up on these and then move on to some others that catch your eye.

Pollard, A. (2008) 'Learning through mentoring in initial teacher education', Chapter 2 in *Reflective Teaching*. London: Continuum. This is very similar to the Arthur, Grainger and Wray book above, in that it covers all the common areas that PGCEs examine. However, it is written in a slightly more 'academic' style.

3

Making the most of your time in school: preparation and organisation

Helen Taylor

 this chapter

- will help you make the most of the time before the placement begins;
- will help you make the most of preliminary visit days to your placement setting;
- will help you plan your time effectively during the placement period.

Clearly during your PGCE you will want and need to make the most of your time in schools and other placements. Your placement will inevitably be very busy, so efficient planning and preparation are essential for making best use of the time and for preventing you from becoming exhausted.

Most of your PGCE placement time is likely to be spent in a school although you may have the opportunity to undertake some of your time in another setting. These may include nurseries and other settings where learning takes place, such as museums and galleries, zoos, nature reserves and historic buildings. Although the word 'school' is used in this chapter many of the points made are also relevant in other settings.

Before you visit your placement setting

As soon as you discover where you are going to undertake your placement there is helpful information you can find out. First of all, discover as much as you can about the school; a good way to do this is to search the school's website and familiarise yourself with any useful content. This will give you factual information about the school including contact details and some idea of the ethos. Make a note of important information like the phone number, address and headteacher's name for future reference. Another helpful website to visit is the relevant inspection agency, for example Ofsted. You should be able to find the school's latest inspection report; this will give you a further insight into the school and its areas of strength and areas for development.

It is possible that you will know of a school or area by its reputation and hear-say. Take care with this sort of information; reputations take time to change. Try to remain open-minded and remember that you are going to the school to learn more about learning and teaching, and that you can do this in any environment. Students on PGCEs will sometimes have been worried about going to schools in areas with a 'tough' reputation, but have then been so well supported in those schools that they can later reflect on the very positive nature of the experience. Remember, especially if you have children yourself, that schools you would like your children to go to and schools where you would be happy working are not necessarily the same.

On a practical note, find out about the location of your school and travel arrangements. Websites can be invaluable here. Remember to leave extra time for travelling through traffic during peak periods. On your first day it is advisable to arrive at school about 8.30am. This should be before the children start lessons for the day, but not so long before the children arrive that school staff do not know what to do with you. After this you are likely to need to arrive earlier, as you will have lessons and resources to prepare and organise before the school day begins. You will need to allow time to talk to teachers as appropriate. Allow for time being spent in the morning queue for the photocopier too!

Many PGCE providers will ask you to email or telephone the school before your first visit. Keep your message brief and include:

- a short introduction to yourself, including any prior experience in schools and learning settings;
- the additional strengths you can bring to the school, such as sports coaching qualifications, any musical instruments you play or particular computer skills;
- ask a few relevant questions, such as what time you should arrive on your first day, what the lunch arrangements are and, if you intend to drive to school, whether you can park in the school car park;
- say how much you are looking forward to your placement at their school.

The style of your message should be friendly but formal. With email use capital letters and formal spelling and grammar. You want to make a good first impression. Try not to ask too many questions – stick to those that cannot wait until you actually visit.

Know what is required of you on the placement before you visit, in particular how you should spend your time in school and the tasks that you need to complete. Schools will be sent information from your PGCE provider or you may be asked to take this with you. However, it is easier for teachers to talk to you about the requirements if you are clear about them. Generally PGCE students will start early placements with short sections of lessons and teaching small groups of children, then gradually build up the time they are teaching the whole class. When they are not teaching, PGCE students will usually observe and help their class teacher, with some time away from their class for Planning, Preparation and Assessment (PPA) and for professional development activities.

 **key points**

Before you arrive

- Find out as much as you can about your school.
- Don't pay too much attention to reputation and hear-say.
- Make suitable travel arrangements.
- Contact the school, keeping it brief.
- Know the requirements of the placement.

Making the most of your Preliminary Visit Days

Student teachers are often concerned about what to wear, particularly when going to a school for the first time. Schools have different (often unwritten) dress codes. It is interesting to observe also that sometimes there seems to be a different code for teachers than for Teaching Assistants (TAs). It is always advisable to dress smartly for your first day and then to observe how other teachers dress; you may be able to relax a little in the future. Male students are advised to wear a suit with a tie on their first day but may find that they can leave the jacket behind or forego the tie later. Female students should remember that teaching involves much bending over (sometimes over very low tables). Therefore short skirts and low tops should be avoided. Many schools would not like to see flesh between a top and a skirt or trousers, or any sign of underwear. It is always advisable to wear easily washable clothing as you will be in regular contact with paint, glue and other messy things! Many teachers will keep an art apron in the classroom cupboard. For future reference you should also find out when you have timetabled Physical Education (PE) sessions and how teachers will dress for these, as you will need to have the appropriate clothing and footwear ready to take into school for these occasions.

Your university will require you to undertake a Criminal Records Bureau (CRB) check on entering your PGCE course. From November 2010 you will also need to register with the Independent Safeguarding Authority (ISA). Your university will organise this and advise you on procedures. Schools in partnership with your university will be informed of the procedures that are followed in this regard. There will be much that you will need and want to find out on your preliminary visit days so you are ready to teach your first lessons. However, you will need to be sensitive and remember that teachers are busy people and that their first priority is the children in their class; you will come further down the list. Choose your time to ask questions wisely, and ask a few at a time. Try to find the answers to some of your questions in other ways. Teachers will be grateful if you use your initiative, so be observant – you may be able to discover some of the information you need this way. Always look for ways that you can help in the classroom.

What do you need to know and how are you going to find out?

One of your first questions is likely to be, 'Who is going to support me?' Different PGCE providers will have different policies and procedures on this, however all providers work with schools in partnership and under this arrangement will have trained some experienced teachers to work with student teachers, to support them and to be a key part of their assessment. In some partnerships this will be the class teacher, in others there will be some trained 'mentors' in the school who will support and assess you alongside a class teacher who will have a more informal role.

Some schools will produce introductory leaflets with key facts and hints for student teachers, and these can be really helpful guides that free the teachers to talk to students about the more professional requirements of the placement. Many schools will also arrange a tour for students on their first day and introduce them to key personnel. It will be hard for you to remember everyone, so if you are not given a list of staff try to keep a record of key names. Your mentor and class teacher will be the most important teachers for you to get to know, but don't forget the support staff with whom you will work over the next few weeks.

There are general points that you will need to know in order to feel comfortable and accepted in your placement setting. Some of these may sound quite trivial, but if overlooked, can cause embarrassment later. There are still some teachers who will always sit on the same chair in the staffroom and can be upset if you sit there inadvertently! In some schools teachers will have their own tea or coffee mugs, with others reserved for visitors. Staff members who pay for their drinks do not like to feel they are subsidising visitors, so ask how and who you pay. Also, find out:

1. Where you can hang your coat and put your bag, teaching resources and placement file in the classroom.
2. If it is okay for you to use the staffroom and the equipment in it at any time.
3. What the arrangements are for lunch.

Health and safety are important concerns in any placement setting. You should be aware of key policies and procedures. Hopefully you will never have to use them, but you certainly need to be prepared. Find out the following:

1. What are the fire evacuation procedures from the classroom and any other room you may be in with the children? (Don't forget there will be fire notices in each room of the school and you should familiarise yourself with these.)
2. Where is the First Aid box kept and who is a qualified First Aider? What are the procedures to follow for minor cuts and bruises?
3. Are there any children in your class with chronic illnesses, allergies or disabilities? If children need medication like asthma inhalers or epi-pens, where are these kept and what are the procedures for this?
4. What are the procedures for children wetting themselves and where are the spare clothes kept?
5. Where can a dustpan and brush or mop be found to clear up spills?
6. Who is the Designated Teacher for Child Protection? (You should have an awareness of the procedures to be followed for Child Protection before you start your placement, either from your PGCE provider or from your placement setting.)

You will need to find out about the class you are going to be working with. This will include their names and ages (especially in a mixed class) and any organisational groupings. This will be especially important in a nursery setting where many of the children may be part-time and there may be different children around in the afternoon from the morning. You will also need to know about children with additional needs and children who are learning English as an Additional Language (EAL) so you can adequately cater for their needs once you start teaching. Your class teacher and the Special Educational Needs Co-ordinator (SENCO) will be able to help with this. You will be able to learn much about the children's needs and interests through observing them in class and in other situations around the school.

In order to start planning your teaching and the children's learning effectively, you will need to find out about the resources available. Some will be kept in the classroom and you could ask the teacher if it is possible for you to have a look through the cupboards and drawers at a time when the children are not in the room. Shared resources are likely to be kept in designated places around the school. Make time to discover these well in advance of needing to use them. Check the policy for expendable resources and for the photocopier. Many schools keep expensive photocopying to a minimum or have an allowance per class per term; you will need to work within this system, and this may also help you to plan a greater variety of activities for children! Time can also be invested in discovering how to operate equipment available to you; this might apply to Interactive White Boards, particularly if the school operates a different system to the one you are used to. Discover which software is available to the children to support their learning in class and possibly in an ICT suite.

Find out about the organisation of the day, the week, and the term, where there is flexibility and where times are fixed. Some warning of special days or events coming up, for example, Sports Day, Harvest Festival or European Day, will help you plan for the children's interests more precisely.

key points

On your placement

- Be considerate towards busy teachers.
- Use your initiative, for example in finding information from different sources.
- Find out key information about the class, the school, and its organisation.
- Find out about health and safety policies and procedures.
- Find out about the learning needs of the class through documentation and observation.
- Find out about the resources you can use.

reflective task

Think about that moment when you meet your class for the first time. What will you say? How will you act?

Preparing for behaviour management

Many student teachers worry about managing behaviour. Read the school policy and familiarise yourself with classroom rules and procedures. Check with your teacher that you should follow the same procedures and that you can issue rewards and sanctions as appropriate. Invest time in behaviour management at the beginning of your placement, starting in the way you wish to continue. One idea is to revise the class rules with children during the first time you are in charge. Explain that the rules apply when you are teaching, just as they apply when their regular teacher is working with them. Highlight one of the rules: there is usually one about taking turns to speak and not calling out. Ask the children to suggest why this is a rule and tell them you will be looking out for those children who remember that rule in particular. Remember to praise children who demonstrate that rule during the day. Throughout your placement maintain a positive approach to behaviour management and be firm and fair, the children will respect you for this.

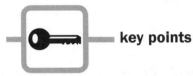 **key points**

To encourage positive behaviour

- Be prepared for behaviour management.
- Invest time at the beginning of your placement.
- Praise appropriate behaviour.
- Be firm and fair.

Preparing for time management

When you are on placement you will need to manage your time both in school and outside it efficiently. You will want to make the most of your time in school to ensure that you learn as much as you possibly can. You will also be busy with things to do outside of the children's learning time, so you will need to plan how to manage this.

Depending on your home commitments, you will need to arrange your planning time. This may mean making complex arrangements for your family, for your employment, and for other commitments. Also don't forget that you need to sleep and have some time to yourself during your placement! It is vitally important that you eat properly; this will keep your energy levels up and help to sustain you. Many students will have only a limited number of clothes suitable for placements so you will need to be organised with your laundry too!

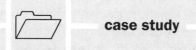

case study

Vicky

Vicky was a PGCE Part-time student, with a part-time job, a husband, and two children aged 10 and 8 years, and by necessity had to have an excellent approach to organising her time effectively.

Vicky was just about to undertake her final eight-week placement, but she was also in the process of applying for teaching jobs for the following term. She and her husband agreed that she would hand in her notice on her part-time job, so she finished just before the placement. Vicky negotiated that her children would be collected from school by a child-minder every day of the week. Vicky's husband adjusted his hours, so he could drop the children off at school before he drove to work. During the weeks preceding the placement Vicky cooked so many meals that could be frozen and reheated for the family during the week that she did not have enough room in her small freezer and a neighbour kindly let her use some space in hers. Vicky would often run across the road to collect a cottage pie to thaw and reheat the following evening! Fortunately, her husband was very supportive and helped out with the housework, taking the children to their out-of-school activities and helping them with their homework.

Planning your use of time in school is also important. You will have certain amounts of teaching and certain tasks that you have to do. These might include observation and assessment tasks, perhaps a child study. Starting these early, even on visit days, is advisable because you will probably start with a lighter teaching timetable and gradually build this up during the placement. PGCE providers usually recommend that student teachers spend a percentage of the week undertaking professional development activities that are different from teaching their base class. Use the opportunities that are available in your school to maximise your development. You will also have some planning time during the school week. It may be that you spend this time with your class teacher or with a year group team. You will find more details about this in the next chapter.

Planning and preparing lessons/sessions

Do some planning before the main part of the placement starts. On your first placement this may be two or three lesson plans. On later placements you are likely to need to prepare medium-term plans or units of work, plus lesson plans for the first lessons in each subject area. Preparing these in advance will give you time to show them to your class teacher, in order that you can receive feedback and make any necessary alterations. It also means the learning will be better targeted at the children's needs, interests and current levels of attainment. Your school should be impressed by your proactive approach and organisation.

key points

Time management when you're on your placement

- Organise your time and commitments at home in advance of the placement.
- Organise your employment.
- Plan your time in school to make the most of opportunities.
- Eat properly.
- Get enough sleep.
- Prepare some plans in advance and ask for feedback.

Preparing to work with other adults in the classroom

You will probably have the opportunity to work with other adults in your classroom and this is a necessary skill to learn in preparation for when you are qualified. This can be rather daunting as a student teacher, as you are expected to manage the work of a Teaching Assistant (TA) or Nursery Nurse (NN) who is possibly older and certainly more experienced and knowledgeable in this particular situation than you are. However, these people can be your greatest allies if you can quickly build up a positive working relationship with them. You will need to understand their role; this is not always straightforward as different TAs have different roles – sometimes supporting one child or a small group, sometimes supporting the whole class. They will also have differing timetables and it is important that you know when they are going to be in class with you and if they will be taking specific children out of the class at certain times and the reasons for this. You should introduce yourself to the TA or NN if this is not done by someone else. Explain why you are there and how long this is for. Be respectful and thank them for the work they do in your lessons. Ask for feedback about what children they have worked with have achieved in a lesson and if you are brave enough ask for feedback on an aspect of your teaching! It is likely that your class teacher will sometimes choose to remain in the classroom while you are teaching, particularly in the early stages. Sometimes they may be willing to act as an additional TA in your lessons.

key points

Working with other adults

- Establish a good working relationship with your class teacher, TA or NN.
- Familiarise yourself with their role and timetable.
- Ask for feedback.

Preparing for an assessment of the children

You will be given some guidelines by your PGCE provider so be familiar with these before you start your placement. It is usually possible to record some of your observations of children's learning from an early stage, even on visit days. You can also do this during those times in the classroom when you are observing or helping the teacher, as this gives you an opportunity to practise skills of assessing and recording at a separate time from practising the skills of teaching. More advice about assessment during your placement can be found in the next chapter.

key points

Preparing to assess children's learning

- Prepare for an assessment in advance.
- Start assessing early, even when someone else is teaching.
- Focus on children's learning and their achievement of the learning intention.

Preparing for being assessed yourself

The main purpose of your placement is to learn and develop as a teacher. However you will be assessed – formatively during the placement to help you progress and summatively at the end to record your achievements and to make certain you have met the required standards. You will need to be part of the process by evaluating and reflecting on your own teaching and learning, honestly and thoughtfully. You will then try to build on your strengths and address any areas for development.

Mentors are trained by your PGCE provider to help you with this and to give you their perspective on your work. Other people in the setting can also provide you with informal feedback to take into consideration in improving your practice. Your class teacher is an obvious person to ask for advice and feedback and sometimes you can also benefit from feedback on a specific point from a TA or NN in your setting. Here it is helpful to ask specific questions, such as 'Did you think my explanation about the task was clear to the children?' rather than the more general, 'How do you think it went?'

key points

Preparing yourself for an assessment

- Be part of the process.
- Reflect on and evaluate your own teaching and the children's learning honestly and thoughtfully.
- Ask for informal feedback.
- Consider any advice given and act accordingly.

When they are about to start their second placement, student teachers will often tell me that they are going to be much more prepared and proactive in their planning and preparation than they were for their first placement. Hopefully this chapter will help you to achieve this from the beginning. In our experience, excellent preparation and organisation often lead to successful teaching and a fulfilling placement: so enjoy it!

 **further reading**

Cohen, L., Manion, L. and Morrison, K. (2004) *A Guide to Teaching Practice* (5th edn). London: RoutledgeFalmer. Part 2 (Chapters 7, 8 and 9) is particularly relevant. These chapters will give you more details about the sort information to find out on your visit days and advice on planning for when your placement begins.

Medwall, J. (2007) *Successful Teaching Placement: Primary and Early Years* (2nd edn). Exeter: Learning Matters. This is quite a short book and you will find it easy to read – Chapters 1 and 2 contain advice on preparations and your first days in a school.

4

Making the most of your time in school: learning and teaching

Helen Taylor

 this chapter

- outlines the importance of professional behaviour in school;
- helps you to understand the range of learning opportunities available to you in schools, and how you can make the most of them;
- helps you to plan, prepare and teach effectively to enable learning to take place;
- helps you to learn more about learning and teaching through assessment.

The main purpose of your time in school on a PGCE is to learn as much as you can about learning and teaching. Much of the time you will be on a steep learning curve. At times, however, you may feel that your placement is a time to prove yourself, and to a degree you will be right as you will need to show that you can reach the required standards at the required times. Nevertheless, you should focus on the learning opportunities. If you do this, the assessment will usually fall into place too. This chapter will help you to make the most of these learning opportunities.

Being professional in school

Most PGCE students do this naturally, but it is worth reflecting on this before you go into school. Remember you are there as a teacher and will therefore be expected to act like one. Remember the code issued by your General Teaching Council and make sure you work towards it.

 reflective task

Consider the professional relationship you want to make with the children in your class.

What do you want the children to think about you, when you leave? Do you want them to be your friends and to like you or is it more important that they respect you for setting clear boundaries and making lessons interesting for them? How can you develop this professional relationship? What implications does this have for your behaviour in school?

Teachers are responsible for professional duties in addition to teaching their class. You will benefit from being involved with these too. These might include playground duty, taking assemblies, running extra-curricular activities and attending staff meetings. Observe teachers involved in these activities, talk to them about their role and help them. Some PGCE students will run an extra-curricular activity during their placement. If you wish to do this, you will need to negotiate carefully with the appropriate member of staff, gain permissions, and think about resources.

Your professionalism will also be reflected in your general attitude in school, your commitment and enthusiasm, and your response to feedback and advice. You will need and want to make effective relationships with other staff in the school. A polite and cheerful student teacher in the school is much more welcome than someone who appears miserable and grumpy!

 **key points**

Being professional

- Display the behaviour you would expect from a professional teacher.
- Develop a professional relationship with the children.
- Get involved in extra-curricular activities if possible.
- Accompany your teacher on playground duty.
- Attend staff meetings where appropriate.
- Attend assemblies.
- Appear cheerful and positive.

Learning through observation

At the beginning of your placement you will be given opportunities to observe in your class. This can be very helpful and interesting as you are getting to know the children and the routines in the classroom. You can begin to familiarise yourself with what the children can and cannot do in different areas of the curriculum. However, observation can be helpful at any stage of a teaching career. I am still surprised by how much I learn this way, even with over 20 years' experience! To make observations really meaningful, it helps to have a focus, to decide beforehand how you are going to record the outcomes, and to reflect on these afterwards.

Choosing a focus may be difficult at first – try choosing an aspect of teaching you are worried about. Identify with the teacher rather than with the children. There is little point sitting at the back of a classroom thinking about whether you would have enjoyed the task when you were the same age as the children; you will learn much more if you think about the choices and decisions the teacher has made and is continually making throughout the lesson, trying to anticipate the reasons for these. Having a focus need not preclude you from noticing other interesting things.

When you have done some teaching you will be clearer about those areas you wish to improve on, from your own reflection and evaluation or from the perspective of a mentor or tutor who has observed you and set a target with you. Once you have chosen your focus, think about what you are going to look out for and how to record it. Don't forget to think about what a teacher does as well as what they say. If you choose a focus such as behaviour management, you will need to look out for the non-verbal cues a teacher uses as well as the words they use. A simple way of recording this means that you do not miss the vital action. Observe the children as well as the teacher to see the impact of the teacher's words and actions. It may be helpful to observe more than one teacher in an area such as behaviour management; teachers will manage it in different ways according to their own preferences and to the way the children in their class react to certain situations. You may observe differences between classes of different aged children; look out for similarities and differences in classes of 5-year-olds and 11-year-olds. After the observation it will be helpful to talk to the teacher about their choices and decisions. If you can reflect on what you have seen, your university sessions and the reading you have undertaken in this area, the implications of this and any aspects you would like to try yourself, you will have made the most of this learning opportunity.

You may be able to observe your class with a supply teacher. Perhaps the children will act differently with this teacher, so you will want to analyse why this was and to take these points forward into your work. If there is an Advanced Skills Teacher for a certain subject in your school, take the opportunity to observe them and to talk to them about the subject. Talk also to your mentor about the observation opportunities available to you, especially in relation to any aspects of teaching you are developing at the time.

 reflective task

How might you record and reflect on the following as areas of learning through observation:

- questioning skills;
- group work;
- the management of transitions;
- the management and use of resources?

 key points

Observations

- have a focus for your observations (you can note other things too);
- reflect on things you have observed;
- observe a range of teachers and talk sensitively to them afterwards for their thoughts.

Learning through collaborative teaching

 reflective task

Think about opportunities you've had to learn through collaboration. How effective have these learning experiences been? How have you felt?

Collaborative teaching can take place between you and:

- another student or a group of students;
- the class teacher;
- your mentor;
- an 'expert' teacher in a specific area.

The balance of responsibility between collaborators can vary. The lesson might be completely jointly planned, taught and evaluated, or one partner may take a very specific role in a small part of the lesson.

 case study

Melanie

Melanie was a PGCE student, who, although having a successful placement overall, was finding it difficult to make plenaries or learning reviews in mathematics lessons effective learning experiences for the whole class. She found collaborative teaching greatly aided her.

Normally Melanie tended to ask one group of children to report back on the activities they had been doing during the main part of the lesson. Frequently other children found it difficult to hear what the presenting children were saying and they switched off and started fidgeting. Melanie discussed this issue with her mentor. To help her progress in this area, Melanie's mentor arranged for her to observe some mathematics lessons being taught by the mathematics co-ordinator, specifically to see how an effective plenary could be planned to enable the children to go on learning in this part of the lesson and also to enable the teacher to respond to any of the difficulties encountered. Following these observations, Melanie and her teacher planned most of a mathematics lesson together. They both understood the objectives of the lesson and what they hoped different children would achieve; they also discussed any possible difficulties and misconceptions. It was agreed that the class teacher would teach the lesson up to the plenary allowing Melanie to observe the children. Melanie had planned an activity for the plenary where all the children would be involved in extending the learning and applying it to a different context, but she was prepared to adapt it as necessary. During the lesson Melanie circulated, noting how the children were working. She observed where a group of children were having difficulty and was able to build revision of this into the plenary. After this Melanie felt much more confident about using this part of the lesson effectively.

Planning collaboratively with your class teacher or year group team can be helpful, especially in the time before you get to know your class well. You will gain insight into how experienced teachers plan and it will mean that you plan more precisely for children's needs and interests, ensuring your pupils receive their entitlement alongside other classes in the year group. As you gain in confidence you will increasingly be able to contribute your ideas to these planning meetings.

The advantages of working with other student teachers may seem less obvious to you at first. However, in planning, two or more heads are often better than one. Students working together even in the earliest stages have been observed to be more willing to try out slightly more 'risky' activities than they would on their own. 'Risky' here doesn't mean health and safety, but refers to activities that might include more resources, more movement round the classroom, perhaps more talking, and potentially more noise than a paper and pencil task where the children are all sitting at their tables. Where there are two or more students to manage this situation, it inspires more confidence. Another benefit is the constant informal evaluation leading to reflection and learning on what to do or avoid next time.

Don't expect your class teacher or mentor to be able to collaborate with you at the level of the case study very often. For them it will involve a large investment of time, as it will take longer to plan a lesson working alongside you than it would to do it by themselves. However, it can be very rewarding for an experienced teacher to collaborate with a student, which the following case studies demonstrate.

---

case studies

Collaborative teaching

Caroline was a PGCE student working in my year 6 classroom, when I was a class teacher. One of the tasks she needed to undertake as part of her course requirements was to plan and prepare a lesson, then to give the lesson plan to me to teach while she observed.

Even though Caroline's plan for the history lesson was clear and well-written I found it incredibly hard to teach. However, it gave us both a wonderful opportunity to reflect on planning, teaching and learning. After the lesson we spent about half an hour in a debrief session with a cup of tea, but we went on discussing it informally at intervals for weeks. It made me realise how hard it is to follow someone else's plan and it gave Caroline opportunities to ask why I varied from the plan in small details and about how she could improve her plan or why parts of the lesson had worked differently to how she had envisioned. For example, at one point I was required to introduce a new historical word to the children and without thinking I turned to the board to write the word there. From this we were able to discuss ideas about introducing children to new and sometimes technical vocabulary and about giving children visual, as well as aural cues.

Sunita was teaching in my class in the final week of her first placement when the school was subject to inspection. A creative writing lesson was planned for the class and Sunita and I decided to teach the lesson collaboratively.

We chose a theme of excuses for being late and started the lesson with a role play between us. The children were fascinated by this interaction between two adults and then held an ideas gathering session of circumstances for being late, excuses and reactions to them. The role play inspired some excellent quality writing and the inspector was duly impressed. Again, this led to plenty of opportunities for Sunita (and myself) to reflect on planning and evaluation; both formally after the lesson and informally in discussion for the remainder of the week. Also, although Sunita was not exposed to the inspector's scrutiny herself, it was still an excellent way of preparing for inspections.

─○━━ **key points** ━━━━━━━━━━━━━━━━━━━━

Collaborative teaching

- Collaborate with a range of other people.
- Collaboration can take a range of forms.
- Responsibility does not have to be equally shared.
- Teaching collaboratively can help you concentrate on areas of teaching that you are particularly working on.
- It can make a more meaningful learning experience for the children.
- Understand that teachers will only be able to collaborate with you occasionally.

Planning and preparing individual lessons/sessions

At the beginning of your placements, and especially on the first one, you will likely be asked to plan and present individual lessons or parts of lessons to groups of children and to the whole class. This can be difficult as you will be following up on another teacher's lesson. How will you know where to start in your planning and preparation? Your class teacher can help you here. They will give you a topic to teach or possibly the required learning objective. You will need to discover when it will be taught and how much time you will have. You will also need to know what the children have done in this area before, what they already know, and what they are interested in. You may be able to look at some records to gain a bit of this information or you may be able to observe the preceding lesson or lessons.

As I suggested in my previous chapter, remember to plan your lesson sufficiently far in advance so you can check it with the class teacher and make amendments if appropriate and also so you can prepare the resources – it's not a good feeling to arrive at school one morning to teach your first lesson at 9 a.m. to find that another teacher has gathered up all the weighing scales that you had intended to use!

Unless told otherwise, use your PGCE provider's lesson planning format. Your provider will have talked through this and you should be aware of what to put under the different headings, however some areas can be difficult at first and you should ask your mentor for help with anything you are unsure about. I was in a school recently where a teacher and student were having on-going discussions about the best way to generate and write success criteria and the experienced class teacher told me that she had had to think hard about this too!

key points

Planning

- find out as much as you can about what you need to teach;
- plan in advance, so you can share your plan with the teacher and take their advice on board;
- use an approved lesson planning format;
- ask for help where appropriate.

Planning and preparing a series of lessons and sessions

In some ways, series of lessons are easier to plan and prepare. On placements where students are asked to teach approximately half of the lessons, I suggest that it's a good idea to plan and teach all of the mathematics for one week plus at least one other lesson each day, and then the next week to plan and teach all of the English plus at least one other lesson each day. The advantages of this approach include the fact that both the student and teacher are clear about their responsibility for the week. They can have an overview plan for the whole week, planning the progression in children's learning. They can plan in detail for the first lessons and then adjust according to their assessment as the children's learning progresses. It also means that the student who is asked to teach half of the week does not just teach mathematics and English but can also get involved in subjects across the curriculum. Access to the school's medium- or long-term plans and records will be essential here, so you can ensure that you are planning lessons that build on what children have already done and avoid repetition or planning work that is too challenging. However, remember that some revision of ideas will be necessary, especially if the children have not touched on the topic or ideas for some time.

key points

Planning a series of lessons

- Plan for progression across the series of lessons.
- Plan in detail for the first few lessons, leave the others more sketchily planned so you can adjust and respond to the children's learning.

- Use the school's medium-term plans.
- Remember to include some revision time for previously covered ideas.

Assessment and record keeping

Talk to your mentor about how assessments are made and records kept in your class and school; ask them if you can see examples. Many student teachers find recording assessments difficult at first. This is due to several factors:

- When you are new to teaching, there is so much to do and get to grips with that assessment and recording can seem like a lower priority.
- On a short placement, it is difficult to see a need for recording assessment.
- It is hard to set up a manageable system, and to find out what works for you.
- Assessment may work in different ways with different age groups of children, and you may not have any experience of what you need to do.

You will find that you are naturally and informally assessing the whole time as you adjust your teaching in response to individual children and groups. It is the formalising of this in recording and feeding it into planning the next steps in learning for all that are more challenging.

When you are teaching a small group of children, plan to assess one of the children in that group and during or after the session to write something about that child's learning, particularly their achievement of the learning intention. In the next lesson choose another child to observe and when you become confident with doing this try to observe and record something about two children's learning. You will gradually be able to build this up. Remember to ask other adults working with you for feedback and to include this in your records of the assessment.

Recognising the importance of recording assessments on an early, shorter placement is also challenging. One way to think about this is as practice for when you are responsible for a class. You will revisit topics during a year and in order to plan appropriately you will need to refer to your records from the previous time. Near the end of the academic year you will also write reports for the children and at several points during the year you will need to report to parents and others. Records are used to support reporting. Teachers need to report on the progress children have made across a year. It's tempting to think that after a year with a class you'll know the children really well so you won't need to write things down. This is true to an extent; however you will need to look back at your records as you will be surprised at how much they have progressed in the year and you will have forgotten what they were like at the beginning! You will also need to consider how to write reports carefully. Find ways of phrasing your message sensitively. Remember that the child you are writing about is someone's baby! Reports are often read and re-read, then passed round to the grandparents, aunts and uncles and often kept for posterity. Have you or your parents still got your school reports? Ask to look at reports written; by experienced teachers and note the way they are written; it may also be useful to make a note of useful phrases that you can refer to later.

On a longer placement when you are doing the majority of the teaching each week, remember to leave records for the class teacher to use for reporting purposes, otherwise they will have a gap in their records.

You will also need to set up a manageable system that works for you. Talk to teachers and other students about how they do this. Listen to the advice from your PGCE provider, as they may provide some recording formats to try as well.

Practise different types of assessment as you can easily find yourself relying on a limited range of methods. In the Early Years this is likely to be observation, but remember to look at recorded outcomes of children's work too. Conversely, with older primary children it is easy to rely on recorded outcomes and to assess as you mark children's work. Remember that the process of the learning is arguably more important than the product. Listening is a key skill in assessment; take the time to listen carefully to the children, probing where necessary to fully understand a child's thinking. This will also help that child to clarify their thinking.

key points

Assessment

- talk to teachers and ask to see their records of assessment;
- start small – plan to assess one child during each lesson to begin with;
- remember you are practising skills for when you have your own class;
- leave your records with the teacher when you leave;
- make your assessment and recording manageable;
- practise different types of assessment.

Your placements in school will take on a variety of formats and will include the time to observe others, as well as time to teach collaboratively and on your own. Make the most of the opportunities by continually reflecting on your experiences and on the learning of the children. This will help you to improve your work and achieve the required standards at the end of your placements.

 **further reading**

Cohen, L., Manion, L. and Morrison, K. (2004) *A Guide to Teaching Practice* (5th edn). London: RoutledgeFalmer. Chapter 15 gives many details on behaviour management, you will need to choose from the suggestions according to the age group with which you are working. Chapters 16 and 17 are useful for assessment and record keeping.

Johnston, J., Halocha, J. and Chater, M. (2007) *Developing Teaching Skills in the Primary School*. Maidenhead: Open University Press. Chapter 5 will expand on the ideas of behaviour management given here. Chapter 11 is a useful summary about assessment for learning.

Medwall, J. (2007) *Successful Teaching Placement: Primary and Early Years* (2nd edn). Exeter: Learning Matters. This book was also listed in the previous chapter. To follow up from this chapter, you may like to read Chapters 3, 4 and 5. These will give further details about observing, teaching and assessment.

Moyles, J. (2007) *Beginning Teaching, Beginning Learning in Primary Education*. Maidenhead: Open University Press. This book will be especially relevant if you are working with children up to the age of 7. Part 3 contains helpful chapters on the organisation of learning.

5

Being academic

Hellen Ward

this chapter

- outlines why those responsible for PGCE courses believe that teachers and teaching students should be academically minded and academically confident;
- provides some helpful guidance on how to achieve this during the course.

Why is it important to be academic?

Teaching is sometimes thought of as an activity that some people are able to do as easily as breathing. They have presence! The reality is that teaching is neither an art nor a science and requires the 'would-be' teacher, as well as the fully qualified teacher, to engage in the processes of learning and reflection. Learning can be defined as a change in experience, knowledge or skills that will result in an ability to do something that could not be done before. In regard to teaching, reflection, as outlined by William Stow in Chapter 7, is thinking about past performance and considering how in the future practice might be improved or enhanced by a change in approach. A vital aspect of being a teacher is to be involved in a process of lifelong learning and reflection in order to make learning irresistible for others while continuing to learn oneself.

In order to create a learning adventure for you and the children you teach, learning needs to be appealing. An important part of ensuring effective teaching, and therefore learning, will occur through the ability to link theory and practice. However, there is an essential distinction between the surface reproduction of 'knowledge' and a deeper understanding of it. In order to be successful, understanding the pedagogy of teaching is essential and this is gained by academic discussion and writing throughout your PGCE.

Research and theory is the collected advice and evidence from a range of settings that provide a backdrop to view the world. The first teaching practice allows growth; to see how someone else manages teaching and learning, to try out strategies with learners and link this to knowledge and understanding gained from reading, lectures and seminars. Generally, it is on placements that true learning takes place because it is only here that theory and ideas can be linked and seen in action.

 case study

Caroline

Caroline had been working as an unqualified teacher in a school for three years and thought she already knew a great deal about teaching and learning. However, her first placement on the course, in a new school, made her begin to question whether she knew as much as she thought she did.

'The first two weeks were the worse, when you felt out of your depth, whilst you sorted out, "how they do it here", and often this was very different from what I expected. By the end of week 4 though, I never wanted to leave. The scariest thing about ending the course was, now I have to be sure how I am going do it, as there comes a point when you have to do it "for real" and you have to get it right.'

These thoughts from Caroline, a PGCE student following a modular route, demonstrate that all schools are different and that teaching is not just about learning on the job. This student found that theory was powerful and teaching required her to manage the learning of different groups of children in a different context. She expected to be able to transfer the strategies she had seen and used in one setting straight into another. Reading and discussing approaches enabled her to understand and embrace the differences and see other ways of looking at teaching and learning: by week 4 she had learnt many things that she was able to take back to her own school. Theory and practice combined can enable teachers as learners to become truly active participants in their own learning process. Writing about your experiences, with reference to them and the writing of others, enables a meaningful transfer of responsibility for learning away from the institution to you. Whilst it can be comfortable to be told how to teach, what to teach, and everything you need to know about behaviour management, this 'tips to teaching' approach cannot cover every possibility because all pupils, classes, and schools are different.

 reflective task

Look at the web and use your university-based materials to investigate how many types of Special Educational Needs (SEN) labels there are. After a quick web search I found more than 70 recognised SEN conditions in primary schools: some I had heard of, but as many as 40 were new to me. If a 'tips for teacher' approach were taken a student might expect that the training organisation would cover all SEN conditions, as well as how to teach all aspects of the primary curriculum. Would your training course be effective if it taught you how to deal with each of these?

Reading and listening in lectures is a starting point but this will stay in your short-term memory only to be lost within a short while, unless some follow-up activity is undertaken. In the same way that teachers cannot make children learn, but can instead provide them with the opportunities to do so, tutors can only provide the reading list, the lectures, and the school experience. Learners have to engage with the process; by asking questions, debating the evidence, and deciding on their own perspective, on whether these perspectives are supported by others, or possibly on having their original view changed. Teachers as learners need to consider why some things are valued and why some approaches or activities are avoided, and then must use reading and academic study to provide a place for these developing ideas.

All learners, regardless of their age, will differ in their knowledge and experience, learning rate, motivation, attitudes, efforts and investment in the learning experience, as well as their self perception in terms of learning, ability or potential. A PGCE is not just about being successful on teaching practice; it is also about enabling you to provide a challenge and support for many groups of learners for the next 40 years! If this was not enough in addition it is expected that you will form these perspectives and then be able to share them in an academic way.

---

key points

Thinking about your learning on a PGCE

- The 'tips' approach to PGCEs leads to robotic, de-professionalised, and under-prepared teachers.
- Being academic and being reflective are very closely related.

When starting to write this chapter on academic writing I spent a long time trying to work out what should be included. In fact what you are reading now is the fourth draft and this is pretty different from the first attempt. The reasons for the changes have raised some issues about how to identify and condense important aspects into about 5,000 words. I asked some of my students what they thought of when asked to write academically and perhaps their responses might be similar to your own?

 case study

Hannah

Hannah was a very successful undergraduate, who had previously found academic writing, if not easy, then at least a relatively comfortable experience. However, as she knew she would be writing assignments on something quite new to her, before starting the PGCE, Hannah felt it important to review her previous work so she could take a fresh perspective on her academic writing.

'I look back at essays I wrote in the first years of my degree; they make me laugh because they're so wordy. I think there's a tendency (or at least, there was in me) to think that sophisticated academic writing meant wordy, complicated, mind-boggling writing that would take the reader a long time to read and make them feel a bit stupid or like they've got a bad hangover.

I have found a lot of the educational theory I've read for the PGCE among the most 'foggy' writing I've ever experienced. It makes having to go away and write your own essay feel a bit daunting, as if the only way to write academically in education is to use long, complicated words and long, convoluted sentences.

While I find most academic writing interesting, there have been occasions when I have read a whole chapter with my pen poised ready to write down the key points, but when I get to the end I have found that I have written nothing – what can this mean?!?!'

Whilst considering how this chapter would be useful to a PGCE student I calculated that I had marked at least 200 scripts per year and had been doing so for more than 10 years. I also realised I had read about another 50 per year from other institutions where I have been an external examiner as well as second marking in my own institution. I then decided that the theoretical approach was not useful and that maybe a more helpful way to start this work was to think about what I had learnt from all this marking and to identify the things that were often an issue in all batches of scripts. I also researched with my students and gained an insight into their viewpoints. Amanda's case study is not atypical.

 case study

Amanda

On her PGCE, Amanda had difficulties in understanding what was expected in terms of academic writing.

'I felt that because I was doing a PGCE (and therefore had done another degree before) it was assumed that I would know what to write and how to write it for my assignments, even though my first degree was very different to teaching.

Clearly from doing a degree before, I knew things, like the importance of referencing and a bibliography, and to make sure that I had checked my spelling and grammar before I handed in my work. I think that every university has different expectations about the way they want work to be presented and every course has different expectations of content and form. When I wrote essays for my first degree they were opinion based and whole quotes were given within the text and then referenced using footnotes. This is very different to how my assignments for my PGCE had to be done. I was expected to base everything upon research, to reference using the Harvard system, and to use appendices. Even though there were these differences, I didn't feel this was accounted for and I spent a lot of time worrying about writing my assignments and talking to friends about how they were structuring their essays and what they were including.'

Amanda suggested the following from her perspective as some aspects of it would be helpful to consider before you start writing:

1. What reference system does the university use?
2. What formatting rules are there (e.g. font type, size, etc.)?
3. Are appendices expected and if so what type of information should be gathered and included in these?

4. What type of language should I use, for example, first/third person/evaluative or descriptive/based on reading or opinion?
5. The essay structure; writing a scientific/research essay is very different from a theoretical one. How do I show my argument and what I have read to the best effect? Should I quote?
6. The content and purpose; am I supposed to reach a clear conclusion at the end, or am I supposed to leave it open-ended and recognise different angles?

Amanda raises some interesting points which are also common problems I have identified when marking work. Most institutions have answers to all these questions in handbooks, on virtual learning environments and in 'guidance', however students will often spend their PGCE year feeling so overwhelmed by the amount of information that is available in so many different places that they end up not being able to access any of it. The rest of this chapter focuses upon the issues raised. Throughout, the word assignment will be skewed for an academic submission although it might be called a reflective essay or journal in your own institution.

Referencing

This seems to be a universal issue at all institutions and in all types of courses and although PGCE students should know better, unfortunately there will still be occasions when referencing will cause problems. Generally though there are some clear points you can adhere to.

When writing academic work, the work of others should be used to inform your viewpoints. These must be acknowledged, otherwise you are committing plagiarism. You should therefore provide the author's name and date of publication in the body of your work and give the full citation in your references at the end of the assignment.

Generally a bibliography is an alphabetical list of all the books you have read relating to the topic even if you have not cited them within the work. Some institutions only require references to be provided for those texts you have used to inform your work and you have cited within your work. These should be in alphabetical order and contain the author's name, initial and date of publication followed by the name of the publication, the publisher and the place of publication, for example:

Ward, H. (2007) *Using their Brains in Science*. London: Paul Chapman Publishing.

If you are directly quoting the work of others then this should be identified by using quotation marks and providing the author's name, date and the page reference. For example 'learners make links with abstract ideas more effectively when they are experienced through a mix of drama, movement and more traditional practical work' (Ward, 2007: 61).

There will be times when you might want to use a larger section of others' work, perhaps if you are then going to critique it or argue with it from another position. In this case the work should still be referenced with the author, date and page reference, as well as by separating the work from the text. Longer quotations would need to be single-spaced and indented. Longer quotations can also be protected by copyright, which is why in this book the examples used are the author's or from work previously produced by the publisher.

If you are using a picture, table or data from another source then these too should be referenced. If they are protected by copyright you may need to gain permission to reproduce them.

If you are using a reference from another publication and not the original source then this should be identified by using the terms 'cited by', and this is particularly important when writing about learning theory where you may be using a text that examines the writing of Brunner, Piaget or Vygotsky and you have not returned to the original sources.

Avoid cherry picking, even if the quote you want would be more effective when changed to suit your purposes. The following example from an assignment on effective teaching clearly illustrates this point:

> Effectiveness is defined in terms of changes in children's views following teaching, and teaching knowledge as all of the ways in which a teacher helps children acquire an understanding of a topic. (Summers et al., 1998: 153)

However, the actual quote was:

> The aim of this study was to identify the subject and teaching knowledge which primary school teachers can use to develop effectively children's understanding of electricity and simple circuits. Effectiveness was defined in terms of changes in children's views following teaching, and teaching knowledge as all of the ways in which a teacher helps children acquire an understanding of a topic. (Summers, Kruger and Mant, 1998: 153)

In order to use a quotation that had the words the student wanted they selected only part of the text, without reading the whole article, thus taking ideas out of context.

Signposting evidence, using an appendix

There are two reasons for using an appendix: one is to make the most use of word limits, and the other is to attach additional evidence that supports the work. The latter is the one that is important.

To begin with, a 4,000-word assignment may seem like a daunting task, however once underway, particularly if this is a report on work undertaken in school, word totals can quickly be used up. This is the time when an appendix can be used to include materials for which there is no room within the body of the text. This can be problematic because, unless used effectively, the work placed into an appendix does not officially exist. It is also an issue as the word limit is there to support the writer's clarity and if you extend this by placing materials into the appendix you have missed the point. The key points are as follows.

All work in the appendix must be referred to in the text and in more detail than just by writing (appendix), for example, 'One way of attempting to address these issues is the 10 principles of Assessment for Learning, outlined by the Assessment Reform Group, 2002 (see Appendix 1)'.

If you use appendices then all work must be referenced in the correct order in the main body of the text because the aim is to guide the reader through your work, so label the appendices at the end rather than at the start to ensure the reader meets each point of information sequentially (Appendix 1, Appendix 2, etc.).

Ensure that what is being signposted is clear. For example, in the text below the writer is not identifying what was important in a particular lesson plan. The reader should not need to look for the links, it is the role of the writer to guide and direct them.

> It was important, at this stage, to explore the children's ability to interact 'freely' with each other, observing them (without adult direction) when they were involved in structural play (refer to Appendix I – Lesson plan 2).

This is an example of using the appendix as a dumping ground for a range of evidence that might not be needed. The lesson plan did not add to the statement in the main body about observing children.

The appendix is for supporting evidence and is not a place to put valuable information, so ensure that any evidence or information that is needed to complete the story you are telling is included as the reader should be able to understand the work without having to resort to examining the appendix. For example:

> Almost immediately, however, Child B and Child C began to speak to the adult, asking questions and looking for confirmation of ideas to help them move their learning forwards (refer to Appendix II – problem solving).

The appendix contained a transcript of dialogue between children and an adult, all of which was not needed, but what was required here was an example of them asking questions and some evaluation of how this evidenced moving learning forward.

Using appendices well is a vital skill in academic writing as it enables the author to tell the reader what they need to know and where there is further evidence without stopping the flow in the main body of the text. However, if the reader has to keep going to the appendix in order to make sense of the work, the flow will be disturbed and the meaning lost.

Use of language

The type of language used will differ with the type of writing being undertaken. A great deal of what you read initially might be textbook in its style. Textbooks often appeal to the reader by writing in the second person, using you and yours as the form of address. However, your tutors will probably not want you to copy this style in academic submissions.

 **key points**

- It is unusual to personalise your writing by the use of we, you, us, me or my. Many institutions will require the writing to be third person past tense, but some will encourage you to use first person present or past tense.
- Avoid statements that say little, such as 'research has showed us' which in reality says nothing. If there is research then it would be expected that you refer to it directly. 'Experience has taught us', is another phrase that is used in some educational texts and is one to avoid, especially if you have yet to gain experience.
- Avoid colloquial terms such as 'backs up', when you mean 'supports'.
- Be aware of statements such as 'children must' but must they? – 'children must have some kind of interest', what evidence is there to suggest this? You will notice that often writers will use could rather than should, might rather than will. If you decide to use the 'children must' approach then ensure you link this to a writer or theory who agrees with this statement.
- Beware of the spellchecker! This will not pick up errors such as 'site' instead of 'cite'!
- Think carefully before asking your reader a question, for example, 'What is effective teaching?' The reader may think this is something you should be

explaining rather than asking for their opinion. When rhetorical questions are used in non-research assignments, this is an example of the spoken rather than the written form.

Complexity of language

Academic writing involves complexity and it is different from spoken language. This is sometimes problematic as many assignments will require you to relate practical experience to theory, and the practical experience occurs in everyday life. Read the following which was the opening paragraph of an assignment on assessment in education.

> One of the teacher's roles within the primary school classroom is that of assessment. What is meant by assessment and why it is so important has been debated since teaching began. There has been an enormous amount of research and documentation written about the importance of assessment within the primary school setting over the past decade or so.

Whilst this would be fine during a discussion in the pub or over a coffee in the staffroom, and it is easy to agree with the sentiments, the level of complexity of the writing is inappropriate for an academic assignment.

Key phrases to avoid are 'debated since teaching began' as it is emotive and colloquial and more suited to a newspaper article, and 'There has been an enormous amount of research and documentation' ... which begs the question what kind? This needs examples as evidence to show it isn't just a guess or an unsupported statement.

Descriptive rather than analytical forms of writing

One of Amanda's questions, 'Should I quote and how should I use what I have read to the best effect?' highlights a common issue, as not to include any reference to readings suggests a lack of theoretical underpinning:

> It is important to provide children with answers to their questions because this allows the children to gain more confidence in many aspects of learning. It helps children to further their knowledge and thinking beyond the basic planned lesson each Monday afternoon. It is extremely important in the children's development to be able to apply their knowledge to the world around them; otherwise they have not learned anything at all.

Whilst it is easy to agree with many of the things stated here, there is no link to the theory of children's questioning promoting confidence, or to applying an understanding to the real world. Without this theoretical underpinning the work is merely descriptive observation. The use of too much reading within the text can result in just a description of what has been read. Look at the exert below:

> The reason for teaching science at primary school is promoted as enabling, 'children to develop understanding of the natural world and made world around them, so that from the start of their formal education, they build up ideas that gradually become broader as their experience and exploration of their environment expands,' (Harlen, 2000a) and is seen as an 'intellectual, practical, creative and social endeavour which seeks to help children to better understand and make sense of the world in which they live' (Johnsey et al., 2002).

Here there is evidence of the writer reading but no real attempt has been made to synthesise this into understanding. The whole of the assignment was in the same format. These direct quotes have no page references and the writer's viewpoint is not given. This is an example of a surface reproduction of knowledge without any demonstration of a greater understanding of it.

Being a critical reader

case study

Alicia: what is 'being critical'?

Alicia was a student on a flexible PGCE, who initially found the terminology used by her tutors in regard to academic study hard to understand.

'When I started writing my first essay I found it hard to be critical as most of the journals I found on my topic agreed with my own opinions! I emailed my tutor to ask if she had any ideas of how I could be more critical or how to find some articles to be critical of! My tutor's response though was that I needed to reassess what I took "critical" to mean in an academic context. In everyday usage "critical" has the connotation of expressing disagreement or even disapproval, but being critical in academic writing is not about disagreeing or putting an opposing viewpoint, rather it is evaluating the quality of the argument/point of view within the material, even if the writers' viewpoints are ones you can agree with.'

As the case study demonstrates Alicia (and she is very typical of many student teachers) struggled at first with what was meant by 'critical reading'. Take a look at the reflective task below, as this is designed to help you develop a critical approach to reading.

 reflective task

The following is a useful checklist you might want to use when approaching any academic reading. However, give it a trial run here by reading a section from a book or journal you have been asked to examine, then stop and think about these questions:

1. What was the writer trying to convey?

2. Do you agree with their viewpoint?

3. Is the argument supported by evidence, or is it just opinion? (Is there any research cited or links to other writers?)

4. Is the sample size reliable and credible?

5. Has the writer identified areas of error in their argument or do they want you to take it on trust?

In some ways one becomes an academic writer after developing oneself as a critical reader. However, being critical does not necessarily mean disagreeing with others.

Sources of evidence to use

There are many sources of evidence you can use in your work: some of these might come from your own experiences in the classroom, some will be from reading articles and textbooks, sometimes you might be enthused with an idea discussed in a lecture or you might be interested in something you have read in an educational newspaper or publication. At the beginning it will be difficult to decide on the most appropriate source to use. Authors also debate this point. A general rule of thumb should be, if it has been read by other researchers (peer assessed) then it will have a higher credibility than something which has been published on a website or in a textbook. Newspapers will not always state their sources and will write in a way that is rather more general than a journal article. The same is true of teaching magazines, which aim to provide ideas and tips for teachers. These are great places to get your ideas running up and; for example, you might read an article on the use of Makaton in schools where many children have English as an additional language (EAL). This might interest you, particularly when the report says how successful this has been! However, using the questions above you might quickly find that there is limited hard evidence, yet you might also find an article or a name that you can follow up. The more you follow a thread, rather like unpicking a woolly jumper, the more you might unlock the bigger picture. Writing an assignment based only on a newspaper article you have read and found resonance with will demonstrate a 'weak understanding of relevant issues' and show 'little understanding of theoretical underpinning', with the inevitable outcome – a fail!

Secondary sources should also be used carefully. These are where the author is citing other work that supports their argument. For example, when writing about learning in science I researched how the brain works and what other writers in science thought about the learning process.

> Understanding is a personal thing and while it is not possible to teach understanding (Newton, 2000), it is possible to help learners gain understanding by the teaching methods selected (Ward, 2007: 1).

If other writers were to read this and were then to decide to use Newton, without going back to the original work, then they would be citing Newton as a secondary source rather than a primary source. This is less effective, as you are taking it on trust that I have interpreted Newton in the same way as you have. If you are going to write at Master's level, you will definitely be expected to use primary sources.

Policy documents and government information and websites are important if you are undertaking a PGCE. However, it is important that you use these sources in the same way as you would any other. If they are valid and reliable there will be information on the sample size, the reliability and the issues that the researchers might identify. However, some of the newer publications are written more in the style of teaching manuals, with little evidence of supporting statements, research or verification. I could argue that having just one National Strategy for all schools, when the schools and learners across the country are very different, is rather restrictive. While I might think this, I would need to find evidence and/or other writers who would substantiate such a statement. But I can get such statements published, so be wary of the sources!

Journal articles

Sometimes these will have been written in language which can be difficult to access, but that does not make them inherently 'good'. However, the points made in an academic journal will be supported by evidence. In most journals the writer will have had to submit their work to be read, anonymously, by their peers, who will critique the work and make judgements about whether it presents a clear argument, supported by evidence. Look at the sample from R. Lindahl ('The right to education in a globalized world', *Journal of Studies in International Education*, 2006, 10: 9) below:

Who Gets Taught?

If one accepts education as a universal human right, the response to this question is straightforward and clear. Every human being has the right to education, regardless of his or her circumstances. Hallak's (1999) issues of access, equality, and gender become moot. However, this question also implies the need to define the quantity of education that satisfies the right; this is a far more complex question to answer. The expected number of years students will be engaged in formal schooling varies greatly from nation to nation. In Burkino Faso the average length of schooling is only 2.8 years; similarly, in Djibouti it is only 3.9 years. These low expectations are contrasted with 16.7 years in Finland and 16.8 in Australia (UN Statistics Division, 2004b). However, these figures refer only to the typical school-age population in those nations, which is only a portion of the people who would be affected by a universal right to education. The UN Educational, Scientific, and Cultural Organization (UNESCO) estimated that some 860 million people worldwide (20% of adults older than age 15) are illiterate, with two thirds of those being women (UNESCO, 2003). Furthermore, adult literacy rates (and definitions) vary greatly by country, with 70% of adult illiterates being concentrated in sub-Saharan Africa, South and West Asia, the Arab States, and North Africa. Burkina Faso (12.8%) and Mali (19%) showed very low adult literacy rates, especially when contrasted to Latvia, Slovakia, Slovenia, and Uruguay's rates of 99.7% (UNESCO, 2004). Education for All (2004, p. 1) provides very similar data but introduces such issues as the fact that in 30 of the 91 reporting nations, survival rates to grade 5 are less than 75% and a child in sub-Saharan Africa can only expect 0.3 years of pre-primary schooling, whereas in North America and Western Europe, this expectation rises to 2.3 years. (pg 9)

Now contrast this to an article puplished in *Teach Primary!* magazine:

You can quickly improve your science lessons by adding a few lively games. Hellen Ward explains how ... Everyone's a Winner

Do your children enjoy science lessons? Many teachers believe their pupils do, but research into education suggests this might be wishful thinking. And while some see the subject as one of the National Curriculum's great success stories, others are concerned that, over the last 20 years, it has been stifled by tests and testing.

Whatever your view, the fact remains that young learners can find science lessons difficult to swallow, and coming up with ideas to make them more palatable is time well spent. There are a number of ways to approach this, but one of the easiest, not to mention enjoyable, is to introduce a variety of games.

Games can be used in all sorts of situations, regardless of the topic. Use one at the start of a session and children will soon be switched on itching to learn more. Design a game that can be played repeatedly and pupils will be eager to improve on past performances, quickly learning new vocabulary or concepts. What's more, if children work together to improve the class time or score, they will all be motivated to compete without one group or individual winning at the expense of others. (*Teach Primary!* magazine, November 2008)

The first journal article has references to a range of texts and the use of supporting evidence; it uses an academic form of address, and utilises language that reinforces the argument, for example, 'like' 'however', 'furthermore'. The writer encourages the reader to make judgements about what is being presented and there are no unsubstantiated statements. There are also no questions addressed to the reader. This text does all the things expected from an academic text.

In the second text, which is from an article in a primary teaching magazine, although research could have been used to support some of the statements being made, the style is such that evidence is not used. The choice of language, 'itching to learn more', 'What's more', 'all sorts of', is not what is expected in academic writing. So be careful with your selection of words and avoid 'stuff', 'a lot of', 'thing' and 'sort of'. It is also far easier to be critical of the second piece of writing. What evidence is the reader basing their viewpoint on? I would look dimly on students who reference the second piece of work, even if they go on to expand upon its academic inadequacies, as I would hope they would gain a greater understanding of the issues by referencing a text which uses theory and research and does not make unsubstantiated statements using the spoken rather than written form. However, such a paper would not be found in a teaching magazine or a newspaper.

 **key points**

Some suggestions for being academic

- All institutions will provide marking grids and have a stance on the type of referencing, style and form of address expected, so ensure you obtain the marking criteria prior to writing.
- Reading the work of others is a starting point, but in order to produce a piece of academic work it is important to critique what you are reading.
- Primary sources are more credible than secondary sources, so wherever possible use primary sources.
- Journal articles have a greater academic status than textbooks, or professional articles. The style of language you use should be written rather than spoken and where possible ensure that you have supported your statements by referencing the writers you have read.
- Taking a critical response does not mean disagreement but rather judging whether the source is reliable, credible, and based upon evidence.

 **further reading**

Wallace, M. and Wray, A. (2006) *Critical Reading and Writing for Postgraduates.* London: SAGE. This publication is a great starting point to learn about critical reading and writing. The authors are authorities and write with clarity. This book will scaffold your writing and reading processes and help develop your understanding of academic writing.

Wise, D. (2007)*The Good Writing Guide for Education Students* (2nd edn). London: SAGE. A great start to writing in an academic way. It contains short chapters that can be read easily or used for reference, and it contains clear and helpful advice, including how to reference, what to read, and how to express yourself. If you have not written any assignments for a long time, or your first degree was not about assignment writing, this is the book for you.

6

Being positive

Graham Birrell

this chapter

- puts forward the case that a positive attitude can significantly help lead to a successful PGCE and a successful career in teaching;
- outlines some of the differences between highly successful PGCE students and students who merely complete it.

Look to yourself for inspiration

Imagine if you can an old man, sitting on a wall at the side of a road, between two villages. He's not a hugely old man, but he's been around for a good while and seen enough of life to pick up a little wisdom along the way. This is a favourite spot of his as he likes to watch the road and see the traffic and travellers pass by.

After a while sat on the wall a stranger walks by and stops upon seeing the old man. The stranger is clearly a walker of some sort as he has hiking boots, a back-pack, a nice hiking stick, and a map.

'Excuse me', says the hiker, 'would you mind telling me what the next village is like?'

'Not at all', replies the old man, 'how did you find the last one?'

'Pretty terrible to be honest', replies the hiker. 'The people there were unpleasant and not welcoming at all. They hardly talked to me and when they did they were really frosty and jumped on everything I said. Pleased to see the back of it really.'

'That's a real shame', says the old man. 'Unfortunately I think that you'll find your experience in the next village will be much the same.'

With a shrug and a downhearted exhale of breath, the hiker walks on. A little while later another one comes by. Again, from his clothes and equipment it's obvious the man is on a fairly serious walk. Again, upon seeing the old man he stops and asks for his advice.

'Excuse me', says the hiker, 'would you mind telling me what the next village is like?'

'Not at all', replies the old man, 'how did you find the last one?'

'It was fantastic', replies the hiker. 'The people there were incredibly friendly and welcomed me as if I was a long-lost member of the family. They were kind and generous and helped me with directions and local history. I was fascinated by their stories and loved the pride they took in their village. I was really sorry to leave.'

'That's great', says the old man, 'fortunately I think that you'll find your experience in the next village will be much the same.'

Now, I'm not a great one for parables, fables or legends and you'll be pleased to hear that there won't be any more turning up in this chapter, however, when I came across the one above on the internet I thought it had interesting parallels to approaching the PGCE. Over the years as the course director of a large Primary PGCE I've seen well over a thousand students come and go and one question above all has fascinated me: why do some students seem to sail through the course and find it a rewarding and enjoyable challenge, and yet others, on exactly the same course, struggle and despite still eventually succeeding, find it a constant uphill battle?

There are obvious answers to parts of the question. Clearly, some people enjoy teaching, and learning about teaching, far more than others. Furthermore, teaching comes naturally to some students more than others and the latter struggle more as a result. However, there are a very large number of students who, in my experience, fall somewhere in the middle, that is not necessarily a 'natural' teacher nor an 'unnatural' one. Also, by the time they arrive on the course the majority of students will be actually pretty keen on learning about teaching, even if they do find it difficult and a little alien at first. So what about this group of students, the 'silent majority'? What makes the difference within this group from those who struggle to succeed and those who seem to find it much easier and more straightforward?

The answer, I believe lies to a large extent in the story of the old man and the two strangers on the road. Both have just come from exactly the same village and have met exactly the same people at almost exactly the same time and yet their experiences have been completely different. The difference of course lies in the approach of the two people and their openness to new experiences and in adapting their own norms, beliefs, attitudes, and concepts in relation to others rather than the other way around.

Well, as with all nice little stories like the old man and the strangers, it isn't necessarily that simple in real life and there are many variables that come into play on a PGCE that will affect how well it goes for you; but attitude without a doubt plays a very significant factor in whether you are successful on the course or whether you simply complete it. This chapter aims to explain how a positive mind-set and attitude can be a key factor in flourishing on the course; about how we feel positive attitudes can have a beneficial effect on your classroom practice; and perhaps more importantly, some strategies that can help you adopt this approach to improve your development before, during, and even after your PGCE.

reflective task – reacting to events

Take a look at these scenarios and imagine how you would feel in each. Be as honest with yourself as possible.

(a) You have always imagined yourself teaching older primary-aged children and don't think you have the temperament, patience or skills for Key Stage 1. The placement list for your first school teaching practice has just been posted and you have been given a year 1 class.

(b) You live 20 miles from the university. You don't have a car so rely on catching a train which involves long walks to and from the station. Even without delays, the journey to university takes about an hour and costs £8 every day. There are tutorials on a day where you have no other timetabled sessions. It is likely they will only take 15 minutes. The previous day you had a three-hour session in the morning but were free all afternoon. You can't understand why the tutorial couldn't have taken place then.

(c) The first assignment of the course is looming. It's on a difficult concept and something you have no previous experience in. Your tutor has gone through it but friends in other groups report that their tutor spent a lot longer on it, giving out more detailed guidance. Some of the guidance they also got seems to contradict what you were told by your tutor.

So, remembering you need to be completely honest, what were your reactions? All three situations are fairly standard events on any university teacher training course. All of them could easily be seen as somewhere between irritating and downright frustrating and unfair. These are exactly the sorts of events that cause many students a great deal of stress and anxiety. To an extent, I would feel fairly sympathetic, but there are two key questions I would want to challenge you with:

1. Do you think there are good explanations as to why any of the three situations occurred (or for that matter any irritating scenario that you might like to use instead)?
2. Now it's happened is there anything you can do about it? If not, how long are you going to stew about the unalterable?

Let's briefly apply question 1 to the three scenarios: regarding scenario (a) if you're on a 5–11 PGCE why shouldn't you be in a year 1 class? It's only right that you should be capable of teaching any child in the primary phase isn't it? Or in scenario (b), do you know if staff were available the day before? Are you really saying that you've got nothing else you could do in university on that day, say visit the library for example? Or in scenario (c) is it possible that your tutor is also going to mark the assignment so wanted to give you some personalised advice that was slightly different to another tutor's or do you think you or your friend may have simply misheard or interpreted the advice differently?

Essentially, of course, question 1 is all about the ability to see things from another point of view and obviously some people are much better at this than others. It's also about being open to the idea that people aren't out to get you and haven't deliberately designed things to be as irritating as possible because they get some sort of twisted pleasure from it! Developing a growing ability to see perspectives other than your own often comes with increasing life experience, but it is something that most people get to eventually, although to very varying degrees. A simple trick is to constantly ask yourself at any given moment on the PGCE 'Is there a simple explanation for this?' Usually there is.

Monkeys (yes, really)

Now, question 2 is altogether a far harder one to come to terms with. A friend of mine has an excellent term for this. Whenever I go to her with an irritation or complaint about something someone has said or done, but about which there is essentially nothing I can do, she tells me to 'get the monkey off your back'. The monkey is your irritation and it sits on your shoulder whispering in your ear, constantly reminding you of the problem. You can't change the monkey, it won't listen to you, so just brush it off and move on and away. You know you're going to have to sooner or later, so make it the former before it does any damage.

This, of course, is far easier said than done. I can also hear some students saying that you shouldn't just accept things and where would we be if we all did. Quite right too is my response to that, however there are ultimately constructive and destructive ways to feed back and put your point across, but more on that later. Getting those monkeys off your back isn't easy and for some almost impossible.

So what's this got to do with a PGCE? Well, as we've mentioned before, it's not exactly a secret that PGCEs are incredibly hard work and intensive. Days in university are generally packed, either with timetabled sessions from morning to night (literally) or with assignments, reading or directed tasks and activities. Then there are placements. Stories about late nights on teaching practice planning, preparing and marking are common. Then add on top of this the very difficult, hard-work business of actually teaching, which of course will include observations from what can seem like all and sundry.

Just think about what has to be packed in; the government dictates that a minimum of 90 days of teaching practice are crammed into Primary PGCEs and then there are likely to be courses in things such as the core subjects, Professional Studies, a subject specialism, cross-curricular, foundation subjects, etc., etc. The course leaders have to include so much that the timetable will be literally over-flowing. It's just incredible what you will need to get through.

All this makes the course, to use that softly, softly word, a 'challenge'; and that's even assuming you face no major problems on the way. The fact of the matter is this: there are going to be monkeys flying about all over the place, so you need to avoid them in the first place and shake 'em off quick if they land on you.

As a result here comes something that, in my opinion, is the key point. In my experience, negative students often seem to find the course and all its components more of a problem than those who remain positive and forward looking. When the latter do run into problems it is my experience that they tend to deal with them quickly, professionally and constructively, often seeing the process as one that has made them a better, stronger person as a result. A quick real-life comparison of how two students approached perhaps the ultimate PGCE challenge is quite illustrative. It also demonstrates how being positive can help with the golden skill of teaching: reflection.

> **case study**

Emma and Mark

Emma and Mark exhibited very different behaviours after they failed their placements. Their contrasting reactions demonstrated how important it is to stay positive, even when things go wrong.

Emma

Emma had struggled on her final school placement in all areas, but was unable to identify her own part in it. She was very clear that it was not her fault and that everyone else was to blame for the experience. Every slight issue on the course and on placement was cited as a reason for her lack of progress. In her opinion the course had not prepared her for the challenging class she was placed in, and her tutors and school mentors had given her poor, and at times conflicting, advice. This lack of self-reflection and blame is very common for students in this situation, but on the flip-side, most are able to get out of this negative cycle and make the necessary changes in their practice in their repeat placement. However, in Emma's case, history repeated itself and she made exactly the same errors in her repeat as she had in her original placement and when she failed again (thus failing the course) she again blamed all those around her, including, unfortunately, the children.

Mark

In contrast when Mark failed his final placement his reaction was the polar opposite. He immediately announced that had he been responsible for the decision he too would have failed himself. He said that he knew that things had gone wrong and that he still needed to demonstrate his ability to teach effectively. He remained incredibly upbeat and said that he knew where things had gone wrong and would be able to make the changes necessary. He said that whilst not a pleasant experience, events like this can help you grow as a person and as a teacher, as knowing how not to do it could help you to appreciate what was actually needed. It was not at all a surprise when Mark went on to pass his repeat placement with flying colours.

key points

Ways of staying positive on the PGCE

- Keep a diary – there'll be a lot to remember so you'll need to keep organised. The first thing you should do is put in the dates/times of your university sessions, placements, and assignment deadlines. Every time you get a task, write it in there so you know you what you've got on – knowing what you have to do will help you to start getting on with it.
- Plan – don't leave things to the last minute. There will always be lots to do, don't let it stack up, you'll just get stressed out. If two assignments are due in at roughly the same time, get one done early.
- Keep yourself informed – check your university's webpages and your e-mails *at least* once a week – lots of vital stuff will be posted on these or sent to your inbox.
- Reflect – this is perhaps the biggest tip of all. Good teachers think about what worked and what didn't and then act on the changes needed. Bad teachers don't. Most students will just do this automatically, but will end up focusing on negatives – *remember to think about the positives as well*.
- Try and ignore the course grapevine – most of the time it's wrong. Normally people have only got part or none of the truth and what's left over then causes a lot of concern. Get the facts from your tutors.
- Don't forget to save time for relaxing. Everybody needs to unwind and get refreshed – you're no good to anyone if you don't. This will be true when you're teaching and it's just as true on the course. Sort out times for going out and enjoying yourselves with friends and family. Appoint some social secretaries in your group.

The importance of your peer group

Most PGCE courses will be split into groups and something that has always fascinated me is group dynamics. Every year tutors will feed back on the differing characteristics of each group they teach and almost always the messages are entirely consistent. Some groups are 'lively', 'bouncy', 'full of personality', 'engaging', and yet others are 'very quiet', 'hard work', 'difficult to get going', 'lacking in spark'. Given the comments and the way these are communicated to me, it is perfectly clear that the former groups are having far more fun on the course.

Given the law of averages you perhaps would expect the groups to all be fairly similar in nature. Yet every year some stand out as being particularly positive and content, and progress with seemingly fewer complications as a result. So what's the reason? Not surprisingly it is very hard to say and there are a myriad of possible explanations. However, what appears to be common is that the characteristics of the stronger personalities of the groups can often have an influence on the others. 'Positive' groups regularly include key figures who are engagingly constructive in sessions, social organisers, and generally optimistic individuals who act as excellent role models for their friends and colleagues, gently chivvying them along. In contrast, 'negative' groups some-times have leading individuals who are quick to see problems and focus on difficulties. The consequences for both sets of groups are fairly obvious, especially in terms of the respective moral level of the contrasting groups.

When I ask for feedback from groups on how a course is running, it is also fascinating to see the different sorts of comments that will come back. Points put forward from groups who are generally less upbeat are regularly focused on gripes and grumbles, whereas those from more buoyant groups are cen-tred around areas where they feel the course is succeeding or where their response to issues is constructive with suggestions for moving forward. Both sets of students are experiencing exactly the same course and given that in each group concerned there will be a fair smattering of non-course related, personal challenges to be overcome, it is intriguing to know how some groups face the course in a more positive frame of mind than others. Without full psychological profiling I'm unlikely ever to get to 100 per cent firm conclu-sions as to why this is! However, what seems clear is that that the positive groups are having more fun and enjoying themselves a great deal more.

📁 **case study**

David

David was a full-time Primary PGCE with a very positive outlook. Here he details his approach to the course.

'A PGCE is intense, but as long as you work hard, stay focused and enjoy your-self, it should cause you no problems. In fact, I loved it!

You spend a significant amount of time with your course mates and this was one of the things I found most valuable. It enabled us to keep each other moti-vated, offer support, share ideas, and most importantly, have fun. It can be a

(Continued)

(Continued)

challenge to find time to keep up the things that you love outside of the course but you need a life and I managed to keep up my sport, spend time with my friends and family, and never let the work consume me.

There is so much support out there and you must go and find it. The job of your tutors, class teacher and mentor is to help you, so make use of it. I regularly kept in touch with them to overcome any fears that I was doing the wrong thing.

I also made sure that I stayed on top of my work. It can build up quickly, but by being organised I ended up with more leisure time. I found that doing a lot of reading and practising how to teach something in front of friends and family was also very effective. I think my mum and dad were sick of being taught how to do the chunking method in division by the end of the year!

I believe that by continuing with a positive attitude into my NQT year I have dealt with the workload much more effectively than if I had gone into it with a negative attitude. I have found that children respond better to positivity and thrive on encouraging thoughts, feelings and actions. A negative attitude will affect the most important people in this job, the children. By maintaining a positive approach I have had a big impact on the schools I have worked at. I am lucky to have this chance to make a difference to young people's lives. I love my job.'

Feedback – taking it and giving it

Maintaining a positive attitude and a constructive mindset is likely to pay dividends in your future career as a teacher. An excellent example of this is in receiving and giving teaching feedback.

Like it or not, on a PGCE you are going to need to get used to having people offer their opinions about both your academic work and your teaching. This won't stop after you qualify, as teachers, especially NQTs, can expect to be observed teaching several times a year by the likes of subject leaders, headteachers, local authority advisors and of course, inspectors.

Dealing with just classroom observations (and you can expect on average somewhere between one a week to one a fortnight on placements), some students will see the consequent feedback as personal criticism and react accordingly defensively. In such cases, the advice will either be ignored or at least diluted in impact. However, other students who are more open to hearing the opinion of others will be able to see the issues raised as 'areas of development' rather than direct character attacks. In these instances, the recipient is far more likely to act upon the constructive advice given and consequently improve their teaching skills as a result.

True, taking feedback does depend on how it is given. I think most people would like to have feedback delivered in the same way; it would be friendly and constructive, but as well as letting you know which areas you could work on would also let you know where the reviewer believed you were developing well. But where's my part in that I hear you say, I'm not the one giving it? Well, consider two things here. Firstly, *be open about it in the first place*. It is much harder to feed back to people who are defensive as you know the conversation could be edgy. Secondly, PGCE students actually do give feedback all the time, namely to children. Earlier on in this chapter I talked about constructive and destructive ways to feed back. Well, on your PGCE you aren't going to want to be on the end of the latter, so practise what you would expect to receive and make any feedback constructive, think in advance about how it is likely to be taken, and consider if the things you think should be improved are like that for sensible reasons. Learning how to give feedback should help you to receive it as you will grow your understanding of being able to see things from another viewpoint.

Staying positive after the PGCE and becoming a professional

I firmly believe that adopting a positive approach can mean that PGCEs can not merely be survived, but actually become a life-changing experience. With an open mind, a willingness to accept new challenges and beliefs, a readiness to see fresh perspectives, and an ability to overcome hurdles and problems, you will be in a position to learn and develop at an incredibly fast pace. Those too busy focusing on how hard the course is or its inherent inconveniences are, unsurprisingly, not as likely to reap as many benefits.

In his case study David mentioned something that I fundamentally agree with and this was that in adopting a positive approach he felt it made him a better teacher and that the reason why he came into teaching – the children – responded better as a result. This isn't rocket science. I am quite sure that you would want to be taught by someone who is positive, flexible, open-minded, and open to new experiences and challenges. Studies (see e.g., the 1989 Elton Report, *Discipline in Schools*) also suggest that a positive atmosphere and staff can have a beneficial impact on schools and their pupils. So the obvious question for you is; why be any other sort of teacher?

Crucially, these skills are all part of becoming and remaining a professional. Many of the teaching standards you will need to attain in order to qualify will relate to professional attributes (e.g. the QTS Standards in England include: 'demonstrate the positive values, attitudes and behaviour [you] expect from children and young people' or 'act upon advice and feedback and be open to coaching and mentoring'), but while I would strongly agree that you cannot gain QTS without demonstrating these skills, I believe that they should not be seen as just an isolated part of the training. Instead, being positive should be regarded as part of a holistic mindset and approach to teaching that can have long-term benefits for you and your career and for the schooling of the children in your care. Your course will ultimately want you to become a new professional – are you ready and willing to adopt the characteristics and values required?

 **further reading**

Hayes, D. (2006) 'Characteristics of effective teachers', Chapter 2 in *Inspiring Primary Teaching, Insights into Excellent Primary Practice*. Exeter: Learning Matters. pp. 20–41. This is a useful summary of some meta-cognitive aspects of teaching, for example teacher attitudes, pupil attitudes, positive values, etc.

Pollard, A. (2008) 'Learning through mentoring in initial teacher education', Chapter 2 in *Reflective Teaching*. London: Continuum. pp. 31–47. This is a good place to start if you want an effective, clearly written, but very academic book. This chapter looks at early experiences of learning to teach and how to overcome challenges.

Rice, L. (2005) 'Promoting positive values', in M. Cole (ed.), *Professional Values and Practice, Meeting the Standards*. London: David Fulton. pp. 54–75. Easy to read discussion on the importance of values and a willingness to listen to the opinions of others – pupils as well as colleagues.

7

Being reflective

William Stow

 this chapter

- will help you to understand the importance of reflection for professional development and a real change in teaching;
- offers some key points from the research into teachers' reflection;
- reflects on examples of student teacher reflection.

Reflect, reflect, reflect!

Apart from actually teaching, it is probably fair to say that the activity you will spend most time on during your PGCE year will be 'reflecting'. You will reflect on your understanding of theory in seminars and lectures, you will reflect on your lessons during teaching practice, and you will reflect on your overall professional development as a teacher through journals, diaries and a whole host of discussions with other professionals, friends and family. In your feedback on essays and portfolios, your tutors will urge you to be 'more reflective' or 'more analytical'. You may already come from a study or work background which encourages reflection on your progress. For many students, this will not always be an easy process.

The process of thinking through your mistakes, of analysing why things happen in the classroom in particular ways, and of linking that to theory, is key to you improving as a teacher. If you don't ask some fundamental questions about why you teach in a particular way, and how that is linked to your own learning as a child, pupil and student, you could just go round and round in circles repeating the same mistakes. Many students find that they get through a 'barrier' with reflection, to a point where it makes sense why they have to do it and what they learn from it. For some it becomes a career-long habit after that.

In this chapter, you are going to learn more about why we reflect as teachers, what theory and policy say about this process, and what it can look like in practice. You will be able to see examples of students' reflections, evaluations and reflective writing, and consider what makes these reflective or how something could be improved. You will learn about a whole range of ways of reflecting, some of which will not necessarily be those that you are officially required to undertake during your PGCE, but which you may find useful. Finally, you can follow up some suggested readings on reflection and reflective practice.

Why do we reflect as teachers?

It's natural ...

In many ways, you could say that reflecting is an inevitable part of any learning process. If you are learning to drive, to cook or to play an instrument, you need to think about what is going right and what is going wrong and why that is. If you find you are persistently unable to 'get it' or to improve, the reflecting or questioning will continue and grow.

'Twas ever thus ...

We will look later in more detail at the theory of reflection and reflective practice. For now, it is interesting again to note that the idea of reflection and reflective practice is not a new one. As early as 1933, John Dewey, writing about the process of learning and the role of reflection in that, talked of the necessary attitudes to be reflective. These included 'open-mindedness', 'wholeheartedness' (discussed in terms of enthusiasm), and 'responsibility'. Dewey was not writing about learning to teach so much as the process of learning generally, but his work has been very influential in developing the idea and practice of reflecting in teaching.

It's official ...

Although the early versions of the QTS Standards in the 1990s did not encourage or recognise reflection as being important (in a speech at one institution in the 1990s, the chief executive of the Teacher Training Agency at the time famously stated that there was 'no such thing as reflective practice'), more recently it has become 'official' that reflection is an important part of learning to teach. Today's version of the Standards places a key importance on reflection. Look at Standards Q7a, Q8 and Q29 to see what is expected of you.

Ofsted descriptors (Ofsted, 2008) of good or outstanding teaching by student teachers also make it quite clear that this is seen as a key feature. For example, student teachers should: 'have the ability to reflect critically and rigorously on their own practice to inform their professional development, and to take and evaluate appropriate actions – they are able to learn from their mistakes' (2008: 36).

Teachers can't stop talking about teaching ...

Anyone who lives with or spends time with beginning teachers will tell you that they never stop talking about teaching and school, to the extent that it may become a banned topic of conversation! What this indicates is that even aside from official requirements, informal reflection is always taking place, as you try to work out and work through all your learning inside and outside the classroom.

Whichever teacher training programme you are following, you will be involved in reflection. That reflection will take all sorts of forms – lesson evaluations, weekly journal or diary entries, debriefing discussions with tutors, class teachers, mentors and examiners, academic essays, discussions during taught sessions in university or at your training centre. But it will also include informal chats with your teaching friends via text, social network sites or the pub, as well as explanations to non-teaching friends and family. Those are the more tangible ones. You will also be continually reflecting in your own mind as you teach, as you travel to school, and in some cases as you sleep!

You should aim to think of a continuum of reflection leading from informal and momentary thought, through an evaluation of lessons and teaching, to more formal research into educational practice of various kinds. Some of these types of reflection you will need to learn, whilst others will come quite naturally. We will look in the next section at various ways of thinking about reflection in the context of teaching.

What does it mean in theory?

There is a good deal of theory and research in this area, but this is not the place to discuss it all in detail. The relevant parts that we will discuss should help to answer these questions:

- What is reflection?
- When, where, and how do we reflect?
- What kind of reflection is effective and beneficial to teaching?

What is reflection?

Reflection is an activity that is part of a wider cycle of learning processes. This cycle involves first-hand experience, followed by looking back at actions, thoughts or words and attempting to analyse and ask questions about those things. If it is to be effective and beneficial to practice, this will then lead to trying out different or altered ways of doing future activities, which will in turn be observed and analysed. The reflection is in the middle section – looking back and attempting to analyse.

In Kolb's (1984) experiential learning cycle, once an experience has occurred, reflective observation on that learning leads to 'abstract conceptualisation' (or making up rules and 'theories') about the learning that has taken place, and then on to 'active experimentation'. In other words, as a beginning teacher; you do something in your teaching; you consider what happened and why; you decide what you have learned from that for the future; and you use that knowledge in trying a different approach to your teaching the second time around.

When, where, and how do we reflect?

Clearly, this process can be undertaken in a superficial way or in a very complex and critical way; it can be undertaken in seconds or it can take months or years. Kolb's point is that the cycle is built into the way that we learn from experience, especially if we 'realise' it and make it explicit for ourselves.

So, when during your PGCE do you engage in this cycle? Table 7.1 gives an indication of some occasions or 'reflective events' and the nature of the focus.

Each of these events could represent the reflective part of Kolb's cycle. But by looking at these 'events' it becomes clear that these will occur with different levels of depth and detail and over different timescales.

One of the most well known theorists in the field of reflection in teaching is Donald Schön (1983), who was concerned to highlight that all teachers have the potential to be reflective, and that the knowledge they hold about teaching is much more complex than they may at first realise. All teachers, he felt, held what he called 'knowledge-in-action' which enabled them to adapt and think on the spot in the classroom. But if that knowledge is not expressed and reflected upon, it may remain hidden. However, Schön also believed that at

Table 7.1

Reflective event	Focus
Lesson evaluations	Individual lessons and their effectiveness, learning from practice to inform future teaching
Seminar or workshop discussions	Exploring the links between theory and practice, using stories and anecdotes from your own experience, to help you build up a 'bank' of theory related to your own practice or that which you have observed
Professional or reflective journal, or blog	Considered reflection on your overall development as a teacher, or perhaps looking at a key educational issue or event during your PGCE. Designed to help you become more confident in your overall approach to teaching
Academic essays	Theory, research and practice in education – to help you develop the ability to ask critical questions about education, which can be applied to your own teaching

a subconscious level, the teacher was undertaking 'reflection-in-action'. In other words, s/he was actively thinking on her/his feet and digesting what was going on, comparing it to previous lessons, and selecting an appropriate strategy to employ in that situation.

He believed therefore that all teachers demonstrated 'knowing-in-action' through their teaching, most showed 'reflection-in-action' and some progressed on to 'reflection-on-action'. This third dimension was the one which Schön believed was most valuable as it could help teachers 'reframe their theories of practice'. You will be encouraged to undertake a good deal of 'reflection-on-action' during your PGCE. If you go back to the table above, you could describe any of those reflective events as 'reflection-on-action'.

If we move on to thinking about how we reflect, a key consideration will be the way we talk or write about teaching, in other words the 'discourse' we use. Look back to the list of events in Table 7.1, and consider the different ways you would write or talk in those situations. If you reflect through video or audio diaries, or via sketch books, there would be a further dimension. Sometimes you may talk very formally about teaching, for example in the language of the QTS standards, but at other times, you may talk much more informally or anecdotally about teaching and teachers. A third way is to discuss teaching and teachers in more holistic terms, perhaps linked to their place in society and government policy. There is research (Moore, 2004) to suggest that the most successful PGCE students tended to be able to use all of these 'discourses', but in particular the third one, in which they were able to consider their own teaching in a wider context than just a particular lesson or a particular technique. We will look later at other research which gives an indication of the kinds of reflection that are particularly beneficial to your development as a teacher.

What kind of reflection is effective and beneficial to teaching?

When you start teaching you are likely to reflect in an entirely different way from when you are more experienced. This has been described as 'survival, mastery, impact' (Fuller and Bown, 1975). At first your primary concern will likely be just to survive in the classroom – so when you reflect, your focus will rest entirely on your own performance and whether things 'went well' or not. You may become obsessed with the minutiae of your lesson plan, on the timing of your lesson, or on whether the children did as you asked them. As you develop and become more confident, you will focus more on particular skills or competences and whether you have begun to master those. Eventually, you will move away from this focus, realising that your own performance is not really important unless the teaching has made a positive impact on children's learning.

Certainly, if the PGCE is progressing smoothly for you, you may find your reflection developing in this way. It is essential that your evaluations and reflections do focus on pupil learning, and as you become more confident you will realise that your 'performance' in the classroom is only one of numerous factors affecting children's learning. But equally, you may find that as your confidence in and satisfaction with your teaching goes up and down, you may move between the different types of focus, so you may also move between reflecting on, for example, 'did I get to the end? (survival)'; to 'did the plenary last too long?' (mastery) to 'did the plenary stretch the children's understanding?' (impact) all in the same lesson or in the same week.

As you develop a new set of teaching skills, you will focus on the mastery of those skills; if you experience a lesson in which you feel as if you 'have gone right back to square one' and as if everything has gone wrong, your reflections will read more as if you are concerned again with survival or the mastery of 'basic' teaching skills.

You should aim to focus more and more on pupils as you progress through your PGCE. But all teachers, even the most experienced, will occasionally question themselves in this fundamental way. As your skills and confidence grow with experience, this will happen less and less. The more you focus on pupil learning, the more reflection will benefit your teaching.

A further dimension here is that the most effective reflection does not just look at the most recent lesson. If all your reflective activity consisted of lesson evaluations, it would be difficult to avoid this short-term focus. The danger of too much of this type of reflection is that you can get into a cycle of blame, seeing each outcome in the classroom as having a causal link to your teaching. This is why, on almost all PGCEs, you will be asked to complete some will be of reflective diary or journal, in which you must write, film or speak your entries from time to time. All tutors will or should encourage you to take a broader look, and this broader look should include some consideration of wider issues, such as policy in the school or region, research into children's learning, and even reflection on your own learning and personality and how these influence your teaching. Moore (2004) classified the types of reflection students engage with in this way:

- *ritualistic reflection* where reflection is essentially a paper exercise, designed to meet external requirements – the programme requirements, the standards, the expectations of your mentor;
- *pseudo reflection* where reflection is undertaken with the best intentions but does not lead to any change in practice;
- *authentic reflection* where you aim to ask critical questions of your practice and the situations in which it took place, and this can lead to real change in the way you approach your teaching.

In his research many 'failing' PGCE students were finding it difficult to get beyond a cycle of reflection on short-term action and outcomes. He noted that the successful students also moved on from a concern with immediate lessons and issues on placement, to a broader outlook and a greater focus on the nature of reflection and which kinds of reflective activity they found useful. This latter type could be called 'reflexive reflection'.

Reflexive reflection involves you being aware of how you think and react in teaching situations, how you as a teacher position yourself in the environment of the school and the political context of teaching, and even of how you reflect most effectively. A word commonly used in this instance to describe this type of thinking is 'metacognition', or thinking about thinking. In the last section of this chapter you will see some examples of 'reflexive' reflection and metacognition.

Much of the reflection you complete, be it lesson evaluations, reflective journals or academic essays, will be conducted on your own. This solitary reflection is important, but reflection should also be social where at all possible, within 'communities' of reflective practitioners. In the context of your PGCE, the seminar in university is such a community. All those present will understand that they are there to discuss and reflect on education and pedagogy. But make the most of a whole range of 'communities' – the staff room, in the pub with your PGCE friends, anywhere. You may find it useful and beneficial to regularly hold reflective conversations with particular friends or fellow students. These conversations will then enrich your own reflective writing, help you 'get things off your chest', and benefit your teaching in the long run.

What does it look like in practice?

In this final section of the chapter, there is a chance to look at actual examples of student teachers' reflections. These examples show a range of types of reflection and give you the opportunity to consider how reflective they are and if they could be improved. The first three are examples of public reflection – that is, reflection which is intended for a public audience, such as mentors, other student teachers or university tutors.

In terms of written reflections, the first point on the 'continuum' is probably the lesson evaluation.

Look at the example below:

Children's Learning

- The children did really well in this lesson.
- They listened carefully and worked hard.
- Joe is always messing around in English, but he doesn't in maths.
- Some children were not writing very neatly in their books, and did not tidy away properly at the end.

Teacher's Learning

- I managed to stick to my plan and achieve the learning outcomes.
- In the discussion at the beginning I think I managed to ask most of the children a question, and loads of them had their hands up.
- The poster activity was good and I have got some good work for my display.
- I was pleased with the way I used my voice in the lesson. I managed to sound more enthusiastic I think.

Implications for Future Planning

- Do more posters – they look really good on the wall display.
- Remember to tell the children that they must write neatly.
- Keep up the good work on timings!

Now look at a second version evaluating the same lesson:

Children's Learning

- Most children could not remember the word pluralisation (they often seem to struggle with these abstract terms), but did remember the idea of plurals.

- Jane, Hassan and Amir gave good examples of plurals.
- Some confusion (understandable) over f/ves rule.
- Callum and Jacob really struggled to get on with the poster – perhaps it was too complex a way of getting them to the objective.

Teacher's Learning

- Timings were all wrong! I ran out of time because I had overrun the intro and the children took longer to settle to the task than I expected, and had to improvise as the CT was not returning until 12.15.
- Management better – I tried out the wind chimes as a way of getting quiet and they did listen much better than last time. I think they prefer the non-verbal signals first and then my instructions later.
- Must remember to praise the children who are listening and sitting quietly rather than name the ones who are not. That was not working today, as it just led to a longer and longer list of people to name!
- Having spare time can work quite well – as well as the story, I got the children to plan some questions to ask their families about the 1960s for homework.

Implications for Future Planning

- Check timings more carefully, but build in more time for 'bits and pieces'.
- Make sure that the activity is the *easiest* and most time effective way for them to show what they know – the poster idea did not work.
- Keep in the 'rules' and references to other languages – good for stretching the most able, and including EAL children – Hassan told everyone how you make some plurals in Arabic.

 reflective task

1. Consider which of the points made in the first evaluation above are analytical and which are descriptive. How could the descriptive comments be made more analytical?

2. Contrast the level of detail in the second version. Has the writer attempted to analyse why things happened? Is the writer critical of her/his own practice in order to move it forward?

3. Using Moore's classifications, how would you describe the reflection evident in version 1 and version 2 – ritualistic, pseudo-reflection or authentic reflection?

For some student teachers, lesson evaluation becomes very 'ritualistic' – it is completed because it is required by the mentor or tutor and examples will be scrutinised each time there is an observation. For others, it is undertaken with the best intentions, but does not lead to any real change in teaching. Taking this principle further, some PGCE programmes give the students the choice of what to reflect on and ask them to pick out what it is critical or significant, rather than asking them to complete evaluations on every teaching episode.

However, the idea behind reflective journals and the more academic reflective writing, is that they provide clearer opportunities for the types of reflection that Moore would describe as authentic, or even reflexive.

The students in one PGCE programme were asked to compile reflections at the end of each term as entries in their professional development journals. The examples below (Millie and Ina) show their attempts to be reflective.

 case study

Millie

Millie was a PGCE student who had spent some time working in other areas after leaving university, and was comparatively used to writing and thinking about her own way of working.

'It has been an incredibly tough term, but also extremely rewarding. I think that one of the most rewarding parts of this term has been being able to undertake some research on areas that are of specific interest to me. While I have been continually encouraged to develop my personal pedagogy throughout this course, the specialist assignment and professional studies presentation provided the first opportunity for me to really spend time thinking in depth and critically about what I believe is important in education. Undertaking a reflective journal as part of my specialism has been a real eye opener for me as I spent much more time reflecting on my learning in university, both during the specialism weeks and since. Initially I struggled to change it from a being a diary to a more reflective tool, but now I am keen to keep it up through my final teaching practice and my NQT year. It has been an invaluable resource to move my thinking forward as often there are discussions in the lectures and seminars which I have wanted to dwell on longer and I have been able to do this reflectively through the diary. It has been really interesting to track the ways I have developed and built on ideas throughout the diary and how I have identified links between various things that I have studied on the course.

I have also been keeping the scrapbook of education articles from the media which was one of my targets from last term. Although I have found it harder to find the time to keep this up in the last few weeks, spending the time to keep up to date with what the media are reporting about the current trends or concerns in education has served to further evolve my interest in the influence of the government and the media on education. I have, in fact, really enjoyed looking critically at the ways society is affected by New Labour's approach to politics. I have become particularly interested in looking at the similarities between the way the government influences the education sector and other public sectors. I feel almost as though if I am aware of the structures of control that surround me and my profession, then I am somehow less constrained by them.'

case study

Ina

Ina was a PGCE student who came to the course straight from university, where she had studied a subject that did not encourage a reflective approach. After some initial difficulty with keeping a journal, she began to use it very effectively.

'I found my specialism very interesting and valuable. Being immersed in this one course for several weeks was very effective for my learning, and I will remember this when planning in my placement. As I had so invested in my research project, my enthusiasm and work ethic as I was writing it up were extremely good. It was challenging to work at Master's level and I feel I have made solid progress toward working at this level although my professional studies presentation did not reach it. With regards to the reflective component, I have noticed a significant change in the way I think and make notes in class and while reading. It has really helped me to relate my personal experience and opinions to theory and other peoples' perspectives. It has moved me further toward getting used to being and feeling comfortable as a professional. The course also led me to areas of education that I found fascinating. For example, I really engaged with seminars on the history of British education, including political influence and international models of educational systems. I carried out further reading in these areas and many others which had been a target of mine from last term.

The most difficult part of this term was my presentation. I felt that I had understood how to critically analyse a policy, but found that I had not in fact got

(Continued)

(Continued)

the idea. I was disappointed also with my presentation skills, as while I had not felt nervous beforehand, I was very uncomfortable once I began to speak. I want to improve my public speaking skills, because while this has not been a problem when I am teaching, I feel that the quality of my input could be improved if I felt completely at ease. I do not think particularly clearly when in front of a class and this has caused me to make errors while modelling processes. I suspect that I speak quite quickly, which I also want to remedy.'

These are two strong examples of reflection – both show evidence of strong thinking about thinking – or metacognition:

Ina – 'I have noticed a significant change in the way I think';
Millie – 'I feel almost as though if I am aware of the structures of control that surround me and my profession, then I am somehow less constrained by them.'

Although the students are not reflecting directly on their teaching here, both are using lessons learned from their studies to carry forward their teaching. Millie shows how her critical reflection on research and policy is informing her wider perspective on education and how this will affect her teaching. Ina applies the mistakes made in her oral presentation to the teaching situation and turns this into a target: 'I suspect that I speak quite quickly, which I also want to remedy'.

These reflective entries seem to meet many of the requirements laid down by Moore and others for authentic and reflexive reflection, which is liable to lead to real change in their teaching or understanding of their teaching.

A contrasting example of reflection is one which was intended as primarily private. On this course, student teachers were encouraged to keep a 'double-entry journal' – they were advised to make notes and reflections on immediate experiences, be those seminars, readings, or practical experiences. They were then advised to return to those reflections after a couple of days and to reflect on what their immediate reflections said about them as a learner, or how those reflections could link to other ideas or experiences in their PGCE. Millie made reference to this in her comments about her reflective journal.

The students were informed that the journal would not be read by tutors, except where students had used chosen examples to illustrate points in their own coursework and assignment. For many, this freed up the way they wrote and reflected, and allowed them to be more experimental and critical in how they responded to their learning.

The example below shows how Millie makes an initial comment at a more descriptive level on the left-hand side, and then reflects on this on the right and applies it to her placement. The original was handwritten, but is typed out for easy reading.

Session 4 – Learning to Observe

What I found fascinating about this session is investigating how biased we are when we observe. We did a task where you had to watch a video, making observations without making any inferences about what it means. IT WAS SO HARD! Every time we tried to talk about the video we ended up making value judgements or using loaded terminology to describe what we saw.

From the point of view of placement, this was a very useful seminar. The idea of stepping back and being objective of the space may help me to find things that are relevant but which perhaps I would have missed b/c I was too busy looking with a biased eye.

I will try to note the surroundings on a more observational and atmospheric level now.

Even if you are not required to as part of your PGCE programme, you may find it useful to keep this kind of journal. You may also find that looking back over previous reflections or evaluations helps give you a clearer sense of how you are progressing, and of what you value or think of as important at different points in your training or teacher education.

On another PGCE programme, students were invited to keep video diaries instead of written journals. The diaries were largely for their own benefit, but students were able to select key entries and share these with their mentors. The students who took this opportunity found that the video format enabled them to focus more on immediate and perhaps emotional aspects of their teaching and development as teachers. They were able to be more honest about their fears and excitement as they moved away from the formal medium of writing. In some cases, two students got together to film reflective conversations which they then used to inform their reflective journal entries.

You may also like to use video or audio as a medium, or to keep a blog during your PGCE.

key points

For reflective practice

- Be prepared to look back and analyse your teaching, and to ask critical questions about what you have done.
- Try to reflect at different times and over different periods of time – as you teach, after the end of the lesson, after a break of a few days.
- Don't get too hung up on the minutiae of your 'performance' – remember that the key thing in reflecting on your teaching is to analyse what the children learned and why.
- Remember to question your whole approach and the values that might underpin it – not just a particular teaching technique, but realising that when things go pear-shaped, survival is a natural instinct!
- Find ways of sharing your reflective conversations/writing/thoughts.
- Try different media for reflection – sketch books, audio or video diaries, blogs, journals. If your tutors are creative, they might welcome the change!

further reading

Moon, J.A. (2008) *Learning Journals: A Handbook for Reflective Practice and Professional Development*. London: Routledge. There are really useful chapters in this text to help you develop your skill as a writer in reflective journals.

Warwick, P. (2007) *A Busy Teacher Educator's Guide to Reflective Practice*. Lancaster: ESCALATE (accessed from http://escalate.ac.uk/3571). Although written primarily for your tutors, this guide actually has a very clear breakdown of the key theories in reflective practice and reflection, which you may find useful.

http://www.rtweb.info/ This excellent website supports the very good Pollard texts on reflective teaching (2002, 2008) with additional resources which you will find useful.

8

Getting a job

Hellen Ward

this chapter

- provides some helpful strategies on searching and securing your first teaching post.

Throughout the PGCE, students often hope that things will be easier 'when I have my own class'. This starts as soon as the first placement is over and is sometimes as a result of someone saying 'when you have your own class you can' ... change the organisation of the classroom, move children into different groups, etc., etc. Sometimes though, rather than the thought of how many changes could be made, it is better to try and emulate best practice until your training is complete, and worry about your own class when you've got one! The process of getting that first job is often frightening and comes at a time when course-load and expectations are often very high and so it naturally impacts upon how people engage with the course. With this in mind, it is in your interests (and also in your tutor's interests and the interests of your children on placement) for you to secure your first teaching position as early as possible.

The time to apply for jobs comes round rather quickly, particularly if applying to a pool system with a closing date. Whilst many schools across the country will advertise jobs separately, some local authorities offer a pool system. Some of these schemes will have a closing date at the end of January, which is just a short time after the start of most PGCE courses. There are a number of different types of pool in operation, some covering literally hundreds of schools. The LA will take responsibility for screening the applications with help from headteachers and their great benefit is that applicants only need to complete one application form and be interviewed once. Another advantage is that if the application and interview are successful, the applicant will then be given information about suitable jobs within the area. Furthermore, most pools will state that successful applicants do not have to take the first job they are offered and in some areas there will be the expectation that a headteacher and an applicant could meet and refuse each other.

However, pools aren't necessarily a panacea. For starters, usually many, many more people apply than are interviewed (for even fewer posts), so the competition is fierce. Also, although all pool systems are slightly different, some in reality are more like an on-line database, keeping information about the applicants for headteachers and others to look through. For example, one I know of operates via headteachers with a vacancy being given a secure password and they are then able to access applications from prospective NQTs who have registered their details. There are no central interviews in this system nor do they take up references or grade applicants.

Personal statements

Whether you apply to a pool or to an individual school advert, these will require you to provide a supporting letter or personal statement. It is important that in preparing this that the essential criteria are addressed. Sometimes shortlisting will require a headteacher or others to shortlist from more than 100 applications for one teaching position. It is vital therefore that the essential criteria are addressed and if you write to each point in turn, the chance of being asked to interview will be enhanced. If an application is unsuccessful it is unlikely you will receive a letter of any kind. This may appear bad manners but is common practice, so when applying for jobs, if you have not been contacted within two weeks of the closing date, you should consider yourself unlikely to hear at all.

In order to give you some idea of what to include in your statement, in this section I have added in two real-life statements from previous PGCE students. After each I have given feedback from the people you will need to impress, real headteachers, as to the strengths and points for improvement. Also included is the viewpoint of the author of the second statement.

---

case study

Charlotte

Charlotte joined a full-time PGCE course directly from university. This is the personal statement from her successful application to the school where she is now working.

'I am an enthusiastic and committed PGCE student, due to achieve QTS in June 2009. Education is something I feel very passionate about and I would like the opportunity to make learning for others as enjoyable and fulfilling as my own has been. I believe that every child should enjoy school and develop a desire to learn. As a teacher, it is my role to provide a comfortable yet stimulating environment in which children can learn and to ensure that they feel confident to ask questions and make suggestions that will help to move their own learning forward. I think, especially in Key Stage 1, children need the opportunity to explore their environment and be involved in discovery learning. From reading about the range of outdoor spaces and learning environments your school provides, I think this would be the perfect place to help children develop these skills.

Through my teaching placements, I have been able to teach, plan for and assess children in Key Stage 1 and 2 classes. I chose the 5–11 age range because I think it is important to have an understanding of child development across the primary age range in order to fully accommodate all of the children in my class. I am used to using the National Curriculum and medium-term plans of the school to help me plan and I have developed my own assessment methods. I have also had experience with children with SEN and EAL and children who are gifted and talented and know how to provide for their learning needs.

Being aware of every child's needs and accommodating them is key to helping them fulfil their potential. On my first placement I worked in a year 4 class, which had the usual array of abilities and personalities. I learnt quickly that differentiation is not simply supporting less able pupils and challenging the most able learners, but also involves tailoring teaching, activities and support to the right level of challenge for all pupils. The use of assessment information enabled me to: identify the specific learning needs of different groups of children,

(Continued)

(Continued)

be more aware of those who were less vocal about the difficulties they had, and plan to meet their needs. I think the use of focus groups is important because they ensure that all children within the class have time to work directly with the teacher.

Whilst differentiation is a fundamental part of effective teaching, I also believe it is important not to classify children into ability groups too often or completely. Placing children in a range of groups and pairings encourages class cohesion and improves the self-esteem of individual children. It also demonstrates that children are not more or less able overall but have different strengths and weaknesses that need to be recognised and developed. This approach is especially successful in the year 1 class where I am currently working, as social interaction with other children is a skill they are still developing and subjects like science and ICT offer the chance to observe how children learn in a different style.

If children are engaged and inspired by the tasks they are involved in, they are more likely to behave well. However I know that there are many other factors that affect behaviour and a system is needed for managing inappropriate actions. In my experience a positive approach to behaviour management that uses intrinsic motivation is most successful. My school placements have given me opportunities to implement and hone a range of strategies that encourage good behaviour and prevent bad behaviour from occurring or developing. For example, praising good examples of behaviour and ignoring low-level bad behaviour is very effective. Using 'marbles in a jar' and star charts as whole class systems also encourages team work and introduces children to the idea of delayed gratification and long-term goals and targets. Basic rules of good behaviour are important and I feel pupils should be involved in deciding these at the beginning of the year. Once agreed, these rules should be consistently applied, as it also essential that all children understand rules so that they are able to successfully follow them. I was glad to note that your school promotes a positive behaviour management policy because I think this is not only most effective but also provides for a better atmosphere in the classroom.

It is my opinion that all children respond well to a variety of teaching methods and a range of resources to meet their learning needs and styles. The same subject can and should be approached in a number of different ways in order to consolidate learning and this is why I think the links between subjects should be exploited. I have taught lessons that combine science with art and literacy (a recent example of this was 'plant ice sculptures' with year 1) and these have been successful because they have given the children the ability to approach a challenging subject in a different way. I also think learning that has a context is more valuable for children because it is 'real' and they can see the point of learning it.

I think that to be a good teacher, it is necessary to constantly adapt your teaching, taking advantage of new research findings and resources that become available, as well as recognising that a good teacher never stops learning. I read a range of children's literature suitable for different ages and of different genres so that I am in the best position to encourage the children I am teaching to read. I regularly use the SMART board where this is appropriate because I am aware how important ICT now is and also the interactive nature of the programs offers another medium through which the children can be inspired to learn and take part. I recently attended INSET in London on using WebQuests, combining the on-line collections of nine British museums and galleries, to teach different curriculum topics in a cross-curricular way. I am very committed to furthering my professional development. As part of my course, there is the opportunity to achieve Master's credits and I have recently achieved Master's level in both of the assignments where this is offered. One was a presentation on the importance of equal opportunities, a subject that interests me. The other was an essay about the implementation of primary languages, another interest of mine since my specialism is French, and in January I spent a month teaching a French class and comparing the education systems of France and England. These grades mean that I am on course to achieve a level 4 overall and I hope to be in a position to complete my Master's in education in the next few years, using action research from my position in a school.

I am aware that learning does not just begin and end in the classroom and for this reason it is crucial to develop positive relationships with parents and carers. This communication helps the children to progress and makes the parents feel involved in the learning process. From attending a staff development on child protection, I know that these links are also vital for keeping children safe. I also believe that the school should make efforts to provide extra-curricular activities, which offer children fun and valuable experiences that enrich learning and which they may not be able to have at home. As a teacher, I would expect to lead an extra-curricular activity as part of my responsibilities; this might be a language club or sports activity. I should also like to be involved in wider aspects of school life by helping out with school events. For the year 4 Christmas production, in collaboration with the other student teacher, I was responsible for sourcing and making the costumes, which was something I really enjoyed. On my school placements I have formed good professional relationships with the other teachers and teaching assistants, and I enjoy the collaborative nature of teaching. I am excited about the prospect of becoming part of a strong team where everyone is committed to providing a supportive but challenging learning environment.'

case study

Oliver

In this example, Oliver, a part-time PGCE student, wrote the personal statement under the headings required by the job advertisement, something which is often recommended.

Professional attributes

'I believe that every child has the ability to achieve their full educational potential. The teacher's job is to help them to achieve this. They can do this by believing in the children and encouraging them to reach their full potential.

I believe that, although as a teacher you are often the only adult in the classroom, you are still part of a teaching team. In my second-year placement I worked closely within a yearly teaching team, which helped with planning and sharing ideas. In my first-year placement I also had the opportunity to work within a group of students, which allowed us to share and reflect upon each other's teaching. I feel that this collaboration should stretch beyond teachers to other professionals within schools and outside of them, as they can be excellent resources to help with children's learning. The potential for involving parents within children's learning is an area I feel is undervalued, as children spend more time at home than in school so learning should be able to continue outside of school. Therefore, this also involves the rest of the community, as they can be effective resources to use in extending children's learning.

As a teacher I feel that you also take on the role of the learner, as you reflect upon your practice and address your weaknesses. When local and national initiatives are brought in, these should be seen as an opportunity to try new ideas and evaluate your current practice.

Knowledge and understanding

I understand that, as every child is different, they will learn differently. I use a range of teaching strategies to facilitate children's learning. I have used a range of behaviour management techniques in the classroom to encourage an appropriate and effective learning environment. I have a firm but fair attitude towards behaviour management and I feel that one of the most important factors in behaviour management is that it is consistent in the classroom and throughout the school and is in line with the school's behaviour policy.

Within my placements I have taught using the National Curriculum for Key Stages 1 and 2. I have also taught and planned a literacy scheme of work and a mathematics unit using the National Curriculum. I am looking forward to implementing the new National Curriculum, as I believe there are many positive elements to cross-curricula learning. As mentioned before I believe all children learn differently, I am therefore a strong advocator of personalised learning and feel the new government initiative on this is a positive step. I have worked with children whose special educational needs mean they need personal provision, such as two children in my second year that who had dyspraxia. The schools I have been placed in have had very few children with English as an additional language so I have had little experience in teaching children with EAL. However, it is an area I am looking to develop in my final practice and NQT year. The government publication, 'Personalised Learning, A Practical Guide' has information on how to support these children, as does 'Every Child Matters'. Another government publication I feel has real potential in the classroom is 'Excellence and Enjoyment'. I believe that if children enjoy and are interested in their learning, then they will be more motivated to succeed. For this to happen teachers need to consider how children are different and so also need to use different learning experiences in the classroom. On teaching practice I have followed schools' inclusion policies to make sure all the children in the class are included in the learning experiences in my lessons.

Skills and abilities

On my teaching practices I have planned for children of a variety of ages and abilities within year 1, year 3 and year 5. I have created a literacy and mathematics scheme of work and have completed lesson and weekly plans for a variety of subjects within the curriculum. On my second year practice in year 5 I was asked by the teacher to set targets in mathematics and literacy for the children and was invited in my first-year practice to assist in marking year 2 SATs. In all of my placement schools I have followed the schools' marking policies and through this have developed my own assessment methods. I have also used the APPs method of assessment, to assess the different ability groups within the class. The most valuable form of assessment I feel I have used in school has been 'Assessment for Learning'. Using formative assessment to influence my planning has allowed me to become much more flexible and meet children's needs.

In my last teaching practice I had the opportunity to create displays. One display I turned into an interactive 'VCOP' board, which worked as a resource for the children when doing writing. The other I used to display and celebrate children of all abilities' work, as I feel this is an effective strategy to motivate children.

Within my lessons I always try to involve some discussion work. When children discuss their ideas and theories with each other, not only do they develop their speaking and listening skills but they can also reflect upon and consolidate their ideas. It has been commented on in my previous placements that I have a

(Continued)

(Continued)

good relationship and can communicate well with children. I have had few opportunities to liaise with parents but as they know their children better than I do, as a teacher, it is an area I wish to gain experience in.

I have worked effectively within a yearly teaching team in my second placement, in which there were two student teachers, two class teachers and two classroom assistants, all involved in facilitating the children's learning. In my first year I had the opportunity to work as part of a student teaching team. Also in this year I helped run a 'Tag Rugby' and 'Cricket' team, in which I was a member of the coaching team. I feel that working with and observing colleagues is a valuable experience. It allows you to reflect upon your own teaching and see new ideas which can then be implemented into your own teaching. In my second-year placement the class teacher and I tried to 'Team Teach' some lessons. We found this to be a really positive experience, as we were able to use each other's ideas and provide a variety of teaching styles and experiences for the children.'

Feedback from headteacher A

I think that the letters are good. I also think that when letters are read these days that many seem similar and that the job description and answering this is what heads seem to consider. The first letter does this effectively. The second letter almost seems to be an essay, and perhaps needs to make reference more to the school and not any school. Do we want to develop empathy for children from other cultures? We want to promote respect, understanding and celebrate similarities whilst recognising differences. I think the student was right in the second letter to make reference to particular examples from teaching practice and this is good, however, he should have made a more direct reference to some things at the school. If a visit is not possible, look at the website or learning platform.

ICT has not been mentioned in the second letter at all – this is quite a key area now. But there is mention of how parents, TAs and other adults are an important part of learning and the class environment. In general I think a letter that does refer to the school in various parts of the letter makes the reader think that someone has taken the trouble to get to know what the school is about and in the current climate ones without this will not even get shortlisted.

Feedback from headteacher B

I really like statements that are set out in a chronological order of teaching practices – much clearer. I would certainly call these in for an interview and would probably employ them! The letters demonstrate a real commitment to the important things such as creating lively minds and giving ownership of learning to the children. The emphasis upon personalised learning and current issues like APP in the second letter should stand him in high regard. Also, I personally value the ability to work well in a team and the ability to act upon feedback.

Charlotte's viewpoint and response

I found writing a personal statement really challenging because it is difficult to know what the schools are looking for and how to make your statement stand out from the others they will receive. I wanted to make sure that my statement was not too generic and reflected my personality and ethos, but at the same time I also wanted to show that I would be able to fit in with a school community and be flexible depending upon what they were looking for. I was also unsure about how much I should sell myself (because I wanted to demonstrate that I am capable but not come across as arrogant or that I feel I have nothing to learn). I found the feedback very useful because it showed me which areas needed improving or extending, and I think that having another person's perspective (especially someone who runs a primary school) enables you to see it objectively instead of just subjectively. I am hoping that as I have made the suggested changes, I will have more chance of getting interviews in the schools I would like to work in.

 reflective task

What if your statement isn't working?

It's quite normal not to be offered an interview on your first couple of applications, but if you seem to be getting no interviews from several applications it's probably time to take another look at your statement. Review this based on the following questions:

1. In which ways have you made it personal to the school you are applying to?

2. What examples have you given to support your statements?

3. Have you included information about assessment, Special Educational Needs and ICT?

4. Is your personality coming across – does your personal statement express something that is personal to yourself?

5. Is it less than two sides long?

6. Have you repeated yourself?

key points

Things to avoid!

These are from a local authority recruitment officer, who receives applications from across their county. They are all based on things that do unfortunately happen.

- Don't put anything in with your application – headteachers do not want bars of chocolate, photographs of yourself or small gifts.
- Avoid spelling errors – most applications will ask for statements and, unless requested, word process these.
- Don't send in letters that have seen better days – the worst one I've seen had grease and food marks on it. This is not homework, this is the first perception a potential employer will have of you.
- Be careful on length – if there is no guidance then one page is too short and four pages are too long.
- Provide examples where possible, to illustrate what you are explaining.
- Meet the deadlines; applications will not be looked at if they arrive late or at the wrong place.

The interview

In preparing for the interview you should try to visit the venue in advance, to see how long it will take to get there. Arriving late or flustered and disorientated does not create a good impression. Plan well for the interview, but if it takes place during a teaching placement, always be professional and ask for permission to attend the interview from your placement school. Headteachers will understand, and allow time for this. Inform both them and the ITT provider of the outcome.

What to wear

This is very dependent on the school and the setting, which is why visiting the school prior to applying for a position can be helpful. Indeed many adverts recommend making an appointment to visit the school. A judgement can then be made about the form of dress code that will be most suitable for the occasion. Generally headteachers will always prefer you to dress smartly and professionally for an interview. On the fairly obvious scale of advice, incredibly, we have heard stories of people going to interviews in beach wear and nightclub attire (yes, really), but on the more subjective end of the spectrum you will need to make some choices about things like coloured hair (e.g. bright colours as opposed to highlights!) and body piercings. Whilst we would certainly hope that headteachers would take a view that they should accept you for what you are, in an interview people will make up their minds on first impressions and it is pointless to pretend otherwise. One male headteacher in a small school working in partnership with us, who wears large numbers of ear-rings, said that he had removed these to help get his current job; so even the most senior members of schools have to take some difficult decisions in this regard.

key points

Interviews, a headteacher's perspective

These were written by a headteacher who has been involved in interviewing for a pool as well as for their own school. They also have experience of interviewing for both NQT and senior management positions.

- Have a portfolio that shows different aspects of the learning you have taught. Include the medium- and short-term planning, assessment and your evalua-tion. It does not matter if the plans have notes and jottings as these show it is a working document. Point to how the Teaching Assistant was part of the lesson.
- Make sure you have some ideas about equality and inclusion. What do these mean? How do you promote these in the classroom? Consider visual prompts, multi-cultural aspects celebrating similarities and differences.
- Include something you have taught that you thought went well. It is quite good to have this in your portfolio so that when you talk about it you can show such things as well.
- Think about how you utilise adults in your classroom. Remember that this is a partnership and everyone needs to be clear about the learning that you want to take place. Talk about other people's strengths and how you can use these too.
- Assessment is always a key question. What sorts of assessment? How are these used? Remember on-going assessments in the classroom while teach-ing can play an important role here too.
- ICT – it's crucial now to be able to talk about this, not just computers but also music, microscopes, data logging, cameras, etc. When in school gather as much experience and ideas as you can about this.

- Child Protection – know what you have to do.
- Risk assessments – again know about these.
- Training – once again this is an area that comes up. Be careful about what you say you need to develop. It is better to say 'I have knowledge of ... and I want to extend this ...'
- Parents – have some definite ideas about this. Key things to think about are partnership, communication, using and utilising their skills too, making sure that they know what the curriculum is and how they can contribute and help.
- Behaviour – some useful pointers are to talk about how: you would refer to the whole school policy; it is important to be consistent and have rewards and sanctions; positive reinforcement is good; to avoid open confrontation; respect between adults and children; children helping set up code of conduct in class. Have some ideas about the strategies you might use with a child who is persistently misbehaving.
- Special Needs – be able to talk about how you supported children in your classes. Remember that having an extra adult is good but also remember to include how you can develop independence.
- Try to smile, relax and be yourself.
- Ask for a question to be repeated if you are not sure or require a clarification of what is being asked.

Other things to consider for the interview

One vital aspect to consider is that while getting a job is important, it has to be the right job. An interview is a two-way process and therefore although the headteacher, and probably a panel, will be interviewing you to judge whether you are suitable for the position they are offering, equally important is the decision that you are forming about whether this is the place you wish to start your career. If this is a pool interview then be prepared to ask about the support the local authority gives to new teachers and to schools in further developing NQTs. Is this an authority that you feel will help you to develop your career? If you are accepted to a pool and subsequently have a meeting with an individual school or if this is an interview at an individual school, then be prepared to seek answers to the following questions. Will you be happy and able to fit in? Does the ethos of the school sit comfortably with you? How do the children respond to the adults and one another and perhaps more importantly how do the adults interact with the pupils?

If you have the chance to visit the school before an interview, take that opportunity and seek as much information as possible. Observe how pupils, staff and parents interact. Can you take away a copy of the school prospectus/brochure? Will they give you copies of recent newsletters and general policies such as behaviour and equal opportunities? You are likely to have received information about the school already but you can always seek more. Does the school have a website? What does the last inspection report say about the school?

case study

Charlotte's interview

Charlotte was a PGCE student on a full-time course, whose personal statement you have already read. Charlotte was naturally quite shy and prone to nerves, but she wanted to prepare and perform as well as she possibly could at her interviews.

'Although the job advert had given the closing date and the date for interview, I was still surprised when I received a call to my mobile on the Friday morning to ask me to an interview in London the next Monday at 9 a.m.! I was told that I would be interviewed and have to teach a year 2 class. I phoned the school back and asked what they wanted me to teach, they said it was up to me, but it should be about 20 minutes and maths was expected.

I selected a session on shape as I thought the resources would be easy to assemble at this late stage and I had recently taught this area successfully.

I decided to wear a bright but simple dress and arrived at the school early and found there were another nine applications who would be interviewed. I only met one other applicant, who was interviewed whilst I did my teaching slot. I did not have to meet the school council, but the children I taught were asked which lesson they preferred at the end of the day. I am glad that I did not know this at the start.

I am quite shy but I really liked the school and the headteacher and I found myself answering the questions confidently, in fact I was almost impossible to shut up. I had looked at the top hints before and all of these areas came up. At the end of the interview they asked if I was still a candidate. They also asked if they were to offer the position would I be able to start before the end of the summer term, to get to know the school. I said 'yes' to both questions and was then told I would hear later that day, one way or the other.

I spent the next few hours refusing to go on the underground in case a phone call came and I missed it. At 2.30 I got a call from the headteacher asking me if I wanted the job, which I accepted there and then. I am now teaching a Key Stage 1 class and although I feel I have so much still to learn, it does not seem a year ago since I started a PGCE and now I have a class of my own!'

As identified in the case study above, the last question at an interview is likely to be, 'If we offer you this position will you accept?' You will need, by that time, to have formed an opinion about whether this is the school for you. If you say 'yes' to this final question it would then be regarded as very inappropriate if you are subsequently offered the post and at that stage decline it. You'll also have seen that Charlotte like many applicants today was required to teach a short lesson as part of the process, which is clearly another thing you will need to consider.

We hope this chapter has been helpful in preparing you for your applications and interviews. Good luck in seeking your first post!

 **further reading**

Kronenfield, J.J. and Whicker, M.L. (1997) *Getting an Academic Job: Strategies for Success*. London: SAGE. This is a really useful book that contains lots of helpful ideas for securing your first post.

9

Succeeding on your induction

Helen Taylor

this chapter

- helps you to understand the nature and purpose of the induction period;
- considers time management and a work–life balance;
- helps you to prepare effectively for working with your own class;
- outlines what is expected of you and what support you should expect;
- reminds you to prepare to continue learning;
- considers what to do if things are not going well.

What is induction?

Induction is an exciting time when you are a new teacher and making the transition from successful student teacher to a fully qualified member of the profession. Often you will be referred to as a Newly Qualified Teacher (NQT). In Scotland you may be called a Probationer Teacher. Induction usually lasts for a year, but this will be different if you work part-time. Each country of the UK has different arrangements for induction and you should make sure you are familiar with the arrangements where you are working. The relevant General Teaching Council (GTC) websites, which are listed at the end of the book, are a good starting point and will lead you to the information you need. You will need to achieve some standards or competences during your induction and you will be supported in working towards these. If you are working in a maintained school the local authority will have responsibility for ensuring that you are supported and assessed within your school. You can also undertake induction in many independent schools through the Independent School Council Teacher Induction Panel (ISCtip). Ask your school if you can complete your induction there if you are unsure.

Looking after yourself during induction

As an NQT you will be very busy and also get very tired. You will probably experience an emotional rollercoaster. Therefore it is extremely important that you look after yourself and try to establish a work–life balance. You cannot be an effective teacher if you are over-tired and emotionally drained. You need to maintain levels of health and fitness; make sure you eat properly and drink plenty of water. Make time for exercise, doing something you enjoy. Family and friends are important – so set aside some time for them. Other interests are also vital to becoming an interesting and engaging teacher, so try to have one evening a week that is devoted to an outside interest and socialising with people who are not necessarily teachers! Some teachers will establish and stick to rules they create for themselves; for example, to work late at school but not take work home or to make sure one day out of the weekend is completely free from school work.

You will probably have joined a teaching union as a student member; you should make sure that you are a member of a union as a new teacher. Often the union can give specialist help and advice about induction and other relevant topics and there is often a reduced rate for NQTs.

 **key points**

Staying healthy and happy

- Try to keep healthy and fit.
- Exercise and eat and drink properly.
- Make time for family, friends and other interests.
- Establish 'working time' rules for yourself and stick to them.
- Join a teaching union.

You have got the job – so how can you prepare?

You will need to be proactive in preparing to start your new job, although your school will also be anxious to help you to settle in and make a positive start to your career. It would be helpful to arrange a date to visit your school in order to talk to key personnel and find out about essential school policies, practice and routines. Most NQTs will be based with one class and so you may be able to meet the children. Much of the advice given in Chapter 3 about preparing for a placement will be relevant in this context too. You should arrange a date at a mutually convenient time for yourself and the school after your PGCE programme has finished.

reflective task

What sort of teacher do you want to be? What implications are there for meeting your class for the first time?

Many NQTs will start their job at the beginning of a new school term and make arrangements to spend at least one day in their classroom during the holidays when the children are not there. This gives the exciting and liberating opportunity to arrange the furniture and organise the classroom environment in the way you would like to, instead of the way your teachers on placement wanted it. Creating displays in the classroom will make it warm and welcoming to the children when they enter for the first time after the holidays. This effort is also useful for discovering what resources are available to you and the children. In addition you will need to prepare things like sets of exercise books for children if it is the start of the academic year. This will probably be the first time you have had to do these tasks and considered these things; it is therefore a great opportunity to take ownership of the classroom and really feel that the class is your own.

You will probably want to take some resources and information home with you to enable you to plan and prepare lessons and sessions for your first days and weeks.

key points

Before you start

- Visit your new school.
- Familiarise yourself with key policies and procedures.

- Organise your classroom in your own way.
- Familiarise yourself with resources.
- Start planning.

What is expected of you as an NQT?

As an NQT you will be expected to make the transition from student teacher to teacher. Requirements in England, Wales, Scotland and Northern Ireland vary, but also have many similarities. You will be expected to show the standards or competences that you previously demonstrated in order to be recommended for QTS consistently in your new job. Many NQTs feel that it takes them time to be able to do this as they have to start again with a new class in a new situation, whereas they had been confident at the end of their final placement when the assessments were made against the standards. Once NQTs are able to demonstrate this consistently they most start working on a new set of standards that need to be achieved by the end of the induction period and reflect the increased responsibility from student teacher to teacher.

You will need to familiarise yourself with the appropriate standards and be proactive in your self-assessment against them, reflection on your own progress and planning your own professional development. Generally, the standards you are expected to meet at the end of the induction time are a development of and progression from the standards that you met at the end of your PGCE and reflect the increased responsibility you carry as a qualified teacher. The wording of these changes from country to country, but they are grouped under various headings and basically refer to the professional values and attitudes expected, the knowledge about teaching and learning that you need and your professional skills, often subdivided into planning, teaching and assessment and monitoring.

 **key points**

Expectations

- Familiarise yourself with the standards or competences you are expected to achieve.
- Be proactive in working towards these standards.

What support and guidance can you expect?

You are entitled to support and guidance during your induction. This is funded by your local authority through the school if you are working in a maintained school. Headteachers are ultimately responsible here and should appoint a senior member of staff to support and guide you. This person may be called an Induction Tutor, a mentor or a Probation Supporter. Their job is to help and support you in your professional development and they may be part of the assessment process as well. You should take an active role in planning your programme of development.

Near the end of your PGCE course you will be encouraged to reflect on your teaching with a tutor and to put forward some initial thoughts on your strengths and areas of development to take into your induction. You should seek an early meeting with your mentor, possibly even before you start your job, in order to discuss these. Together you may decide to amend them, but this will mean you can start working on them straightaway. You will then need to set up a cycle of regular meetings to discuss your progress and review targets throughout the year.

Your teaching will be observed at intervals during your first year – normally the first observation will be within the first four weeks and then every six to eight weeks. You should always know when these observations are going to take place and you should also be part of the planning process, deciding on the focus. You should lead the discussion following the observation. The main purpose of the observations is for formative assessment, to enable you and your mentor to identify strengths and areas for development. However, evidence from observations can also be used to show your attainment of the standards at appropriate times.

You should expect a lighter teaching timetable than more experienced teachers. This will be designed to give you time that is specifically for professional development and in addition to your PPA time. Professional development time should be used flexibly and will not necessarily be at the same time and for the same length of time each week. This therefore allows you to use it in different ways. You may wish to:

- go on a short course;
- observe an experienced teacher either in your own school or in another;
- read relevant documentation or publications;
- have a professional conversation;
- watch a relevant TV programme or video;
- go to an NQT meeting;
- work collaboratively alongside another teacher;
- shadow another teacher for a particular role;

- lead a staff development workshop;
- consider anything else designed to promote your professional development.

 **key points**

Professional development

- Take a leading role in planning your professional development.
- Be prepared for observations of your teaching.
- Lead post-observation discussion.
- Avail yourself of a range of professional development opportunities.

Lesson observations

As well as lesson observations to support your professional development as an NQT, you will probably be observed for other purposes too. These may include routine observations undertaken by the headteacher and senior management as part of their monitoring of learning and teaching. Subject leaders or other co-ordinators may also observe lessons in your classroom periodically. However, the burden of lesson observations should not become too great, so you should speak to your mentor or headteacher if you are feeling overwhelmed. Many schools will try to protect you from some of the more general observations. Your school may be subject to inspection during your induction year and hence it is possible that you will be observed by an inspector.

You should make sure you always understand the purpose of observations and how they are going to be recorded. Recording styles and templates are likely to be different from those you were used to from your PGCE. Generally, you should know when observations are going to happen, although during inspections, you should expect to be observed at any time during the inspection period. Prepare carefully for observation. It is natural to be nervous. Plan your lesson in more detail than normal in case your mind goes blank. Have a copy of your written plan ready for the observer, but do not worry about deviating from it, if you feel something is more appropriate for the children's learning. You will be able to justify this later in conversation.

key points

Lesson observations

- Be clear about the purpose.
- Plan and prepare well.
- Be prepared to deviate from your written plan if this is appropriate for the children's learning.

Non-teaching commitments

As a new teacher, it is easy to feel overwhelmed with work directly related to your class and located within your classroom. However, you are also a member of the school team and you will need to devote time to that. You may find this hugely beneficial and supportive. Do not feel that you have nothing to offer as everyone else is much more experienced. Often you'll find that more established staff members will be interested in the newer ideas you bring and will welcome the chance to help and support you informally. You will have expertise and knowledge you can share with others; this may come from observations you have made, things you have tried in your PGCE placement schools from your studies, previous employment or life experience. For example, you may have a good grasp of another language and so you might be able to help and advise other teachers on implementing some activities in language lessons. Try to go to the staffroom for a short time each day when others are likely to be there – often this might be the last 15 or 20 minutes of the lunch break.

Contribute to staff meetings when possible. You are likely to meet staff in different groupings depending on a number of factors including the size of the school. NQTs will often feel comfortable at first contributing to smaller meetings of perhaps their year group or key stage teachers.

You will also be leading the small team of adults who work in your classroom. This may include one or more full- or part-time Teaching Assistants, Nursery Nurses, teenagers on work placements and volunteers. See Chapter 3 for more guidance in this area, as many of the ideas that applied to placement will apply equally in your new job.

Working with parents and carers is almost certainly going to be a challenge for you as a new teacher. You will want to build friendly but professional relationships with the parents of the children you teach. The first contacts you have with parents are likely to be informal and similar to contacts that you had during your PGCE. Maintain a positive approach, be respectful, and remember that you will be able to learn from parents in order to help their child more effectively.

Hopefully you will also have had more formal contact with parents during your PGCE; perhaps you were lucky enough to sit in on a parents evening, to observe your class teacher when interacting with parents or to have a go at report writing. You will need to prepare well for when you do these things for the first time in your post. Keeping good records of children's learning is an excellent way of doing this. Make notes of what you want to say. At the end of a long day of teaching followed by three hours of talking to different sets of parents, it's helpful to have these notes to jog your memory and avoid a situation where you go blank or begin to talk about the wrong child! Try to start and end a conversation on a positive note and use terms like 'areas for development' or 'targets' to indicate more negative aspects. Get advice from your mentor before undertaking these events; run through what you are going to say if you suspect that a particular interview might be uncomfortable.

When you need to write reports, usually at the end of the school year, read previously written ones. Many schools use comment banks if you are required to do this; make sure you read through these thoroughly to ensure that there are no errors and that they do not sound too impersonal. Refer back to Chapter 4 for more detail.

If a parent comes to see you unexpectedly and you are unsure how to deal with the situation, ask them to take a seat and tell them that you are just going to ask a senior member of staff to come and help you. As you go to find the other member of staff and walk back with them you can apprise them briefly of your understanding of the situation. Another approach is to listen to and note the parent's concerns. Say you will look into the situation and arrange to see them again in a day or two so that you can think things over and gain advice.

It is a good idea to join in with the Parent Teacher Association or similar activities if you can – parents will appreciate this and you can demonstrate your approachability whilst remaining professional. Beware of letting your hair down too much at the quiz evening or other events though. You do not want parents to think that a wild person who drinks too much is in charge of their child's learning!

You will have various other non-teaching commitments in school as well; these will include playground duty and may also include lunch duty, taking assembly, or leading an extra-curricular activity or club. These are all good opportunities for getting to know children in different circumstances.

Some of these duties you will have to undertake right from the start, others you may be able to take on at a later date, once you are beginning to feel more settled. Playground duty is likely to be something you will have to get to grips with early on. Make sure you know the rules and routines for this before you start; if possible shadow another teacher before you take on this responsibility for the first time and talk through some 'what if' situations with your mentor as well.

 **key points**

Fitting in and working with other adults including parents

- Devote time to becoming a member of the staff team.
- Be brave, put your ideas forward, share your expertise.
- Go into the staffroom, chat to staff informally.
- Plan for effective relationships in your classroom team.
- Build friendly, professional relationships with parents and carers.
- Keep effective records of children's progress.
- Ask experienced colleagues for advice.
- Read reports written by other teachers.
- Check reports through carefully.
- Play for time and seek help if you have an awkward situation.
- Be well briefed for other non-teaching duties.

Continuing to learn

You will learn much just through being a teacher. Continue to reflect on your teaching and the children's learning, though not necessarily in writing. Reflection will help you to learn from practical classroom experiences. You should also reflect on other types of professional development activities to find ways to continually improve your practice. You will discover that this is compulsory as it will be part of the standards you are aiming to meet by the end of your induction period. All teachers, no matter how experienced, are continually learning and developing their practice. Of course, the more you improve your practice, the better it will be for the children you are working with.

Increasingly you will be offered the chance to study at Master's level to complement the work you are doing in school. Many students will have gained credits towards Master's level through the PGCE and this is one way of gaining more and working towards an MA or other award such as the Master's in Teaching and Learning (MTL) which is being gradually introduced across England and may become compulsory in future. Studying at this level can support your reflection and further your professional development, by enabling you to read and discuss theory to support the practice you are implementing, and by encouraging you to think critically within a professional framework.

 case study

Joe

Joe had enjoyed and appreciated studying at a higher level during his PGCE and gaining Master's level credits in recognition of this.

Joe was keen to study for an MA and was pleased that the local university offered an MA module specifically designed for NQTs to complement the work they were doing in the classroom and their general professional development. NQTs were asked to choose one of the areas they were working on and to research and reflect on their own practice in this particular area, supported by seminars and tutorials. Joe found it hard at some points during the year to fit in the extra reading that was required – this was especially true when he was writing reports for the children in his class and had also offered to help with coaching the rounders team and with sports day. However, he persevered and was able to carry out his action plan and collect the necessary data. He wrote the project report in the summer holidays. Having completed the work, Joe also wrote that 'I feel that my NQT year has been a very positive experience, and completing this assignment has forced me to be more formally reflective and therefore benefit more from the year than I would otherwise have done. I have taken responsibility for my own professional development right from the start and this will stand me in good stead for next year'.

Keeping a record of your professional development is good practice and may be used as evidence to assist the progression of your career. You do not need too much detail, but the date of the professional development event, the title of the event, and a brief comment can be helpful.

key points

Continuing to learn

- Continue to reflect on your work.
- Use this to help you improve.
- Take the opportunity to study at Master's level if you can.
- Keep a record of your professional development.

What should you do if things are not going well?

It has been emphasised several times in the preceding paragraphs that you should take the lead in your own professional development. You should ensure you get the support you need and deserve; if you feel this is not happening then you need to raise issues in a professional way with your mentor, then with the headteacher. If you are still feeling unsupported you must approach your local authority which should have a named person responsible for supporting NQTs. It is also advisable to seek support from your union.

If things are not going well, this must be highlighted at an early stage and you should be given extra help and support. Any judgements have to be based on evidence and you can help with this by supplying evidence where appropriate. Targets should be agreed between your mentor or headteacher and yourself and you should work towards achieving these targets with the help and support of others.

Occasionally the induction period may be extended if it is felt that an NQT has not had sufficient opportunity to demonstrate their attainment of the standards, but this is usually due to a prolonged period of illness. The percentage of NQTs who fail and are not allowed to continue teaching in a maintained school after their induction year or equivalent is extremely low. There is a complaints procedure; details and support can be accessed from your GTC and union. Keep a positive attitude – or at least appear positive – as this will help you to achieve your aims.

key points

When things go wrong

- Make sure you get extra support.
- Be proactive in producing evidence.
- Work towards the targets set.
- Seek the help of your local authority and union where appropriate.
- Keep positive.

As a new and inexperienced teacher you will work hard, learn much, have many ups and some downs. Remember the values, beliefs and motivations that were important to you when you made the decision to teach. Best wishes for your teaching career!

further reading

Bubb, S. (2007) *Successful Induction for New Teachers: A Guide for NQTs and Induction Tutors, Co-ordinators and Mentors.* London: Paul Chapman. Again, this is mainly relevant to the English context but has helpful checklists and some interesting anecdotes.

Holmes, E. (2009) *The Newly Qualified Teacher's Handbook* (2nd edn). Abingdon: Routledge. Chapters 3, 4, 7, 8 and 10 are especially relevant; however this book is written specifically for the English context.

Pollard, A. (2008) *Reflective Teaching* (3rd edn). London: Continuum. Chapter 16 has an emphasis on learning as a new teacher. Many students may have already come across this comprehensive book on the PGCE.

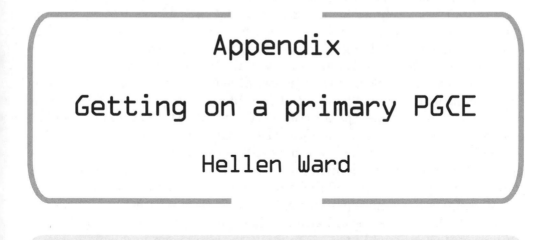

Appendix

Getting on a primary PGCE

Hellen Ward

this section

* will help you to think about which course is the right one for you, and provide some helpful strategies for ways to secure your place.

The minimum requirements

To be a teacher you will need a degree and Qualified Teacher Status. One of the quickest ways of finding which is the correct course for you is to look on the TDA website. As Graham Birrell stated in the opening chapter, there are many different types of teacher training course and clearly the one you take should be specific to the age group you wish to teach. The option that is right for you (e.g. full/part-time or flexible) will also depend on your circumstances. All courses cover the principles of teaching along with practical experience in the classroom.

In this time of public accountability there is the equivalence of league tables for ITT providers on the TDA website. These tables include information about important factors such as the location, grading and number of courses. *There are 236 providers, with 132 providers offering a traditional course and 35 offering flexible routes.* There are 27 institutions providing ITT that have been designated Grade A providers, which is the highest TDA category for quality and based upon the latest Ofsted inspection information. This website also shows the required qualification for each institution and this information may help you target your application. For a PGCE you will always need to have a first degree, and most institutions require this to be a minimum of a second class. Other basic requirements for you are GCSE passes at C or above in English, mathematics and science. If you have not attained these, although some institutions will offer equivalence tests, it is still recommended that you gain these qualifications. Discuss this with the admissions office at the institution of your choice. Some institutions will look at other factors in addition to academic qualifications, so do read any information you find, for example on their website or in their prospectus, very carefully. Don't assume all providers are asking for the same qualifications or experience.

All of the courses available will have different delivery modes and will be designed to suit different individual needs. Go to the websites of the institutions you are interested in and find out what is unique about the courses they are offering. Even at the same institution many different routes are likely to be offered. Many websites will also provide you with a personal email or telephone contact to enable you to find out more information. This is worth doing as you can then be sure a particular course could meet your needs.

Another way to find the right course for you is to use the Graduate Teacher Training Registry (GTTR) website. To get on many courses you will need to apply to this organisation and you can also find the most appropriate course for you by using their search engine. However if you wish to undertake a flexible or part-time route you will usually be able to apply directly to the institution concerned.

Experience

As Graham stated in Chapter 2, it is highly unlikely that you would be offered an interview unless you can demonstrate some previous experience in school. There are no hard rules about the amount or type of experience needed, but generally writing 'I spent a few days in a classroom and liked it' will not be sufficient. Some institutions will require more than 30 days whilst others will expect a minimum of two weeks. You will have 20 lines free on the GTTR application form to write about your school experience. Remember to add other experiences, for example, teaching sports, taking part in a play-scheme, being involved in a children's drama group, or running/supporting a young persons' uniformed organisation such as the Brownies, Cubs, Guides or Scouts. Ensure the experience is recent and relevant and don't just assume because you write, 'I hear children read at my local primary school', and think this is wonderful that this will be sufficient. What is important is, 'How often?' 'For how long did you participate?' 'What are the skills needed?' and 'How does this suggest you have an aptitude for teaching?'

key points

How to get some experience

If you have very limited experience here are some things you could take part in:

- Student Associates Scheme (SAS) where you will work alongside a qualified teacher. This is a TDA initiative and there is money for each day spent in school as well as training about schools and education.
- Undergraduate Ambassadors Scheme (UAS): if you are a science, technology, engineering, mathematics (STEM) or modern languages undergraduate, your department may offer a classroom-based module. If you are studying STEM subjects you can enrol as a STEM ambassador with www.stemnet.org.uk
- Open Schools Programme (OSP): there are more than 700 schools who offer the opportunity to see what teaching is like. Contact the TDA for those in your area.
- Open days and taster courses are run from most institutions. Check with the TDA and your local provider for more information.
- Voluntary work: could you work as a mentor for a student or groups of students?
- Paid work: could you work as a lunch time assistant or a Teaching Assistant? This might be a very effective use of a gap year and would definitely show that you are committed to the teaching profession.

On the GTTR website you will be expected to provide information about yourself and a user ID will be generated as a result. Applying through the GTTR website is an on-line process that you can return to again and again, so you do not need to complete the whole application in one sitting. You can apply for two primary teaching courses and you must put them in order of preference as the form is sent to each provider in turn. You need to have the application completed by the 1 December of the year *before* you wish the course to begin, but it is best to complete the form as early as you can as many institutions fill up quickly. If you are not offered an interview at either of your chosen institutions, there is also a clearing process. There is a fee to use the GTTR systems, so check with them for the current price.

Personal statement

This is an important document. It is your reason for wanting to be a teacher. Avoid bland and obvious statements such as, 'it is worthwhile', 'it is a vocation',

'I like children', because this provides no substance to your application. Also be careful with statements that might make the reader wonder about you, but not necessarily in a positive way; 'I have always wanted to be a teacher since I played with my dolls as a 5-year-old'. Learners are real people and only have one chance; you only have 47 lines so make them count! The system also has a way of identifying statements that are not the students' own work, so do not get caught out! For further advice, the TDA website can provide a support service for writing personal statements.

 **key points**

Writing a good personal statement

Here are some things you should think about:

- Try and address the following questions: why do you want to be a teacher (without saying you want to make a difference!)?; what skills and attributes do you have that will make you suitable as a teacher?; what experience do you have and what have you learnt from that experience?
- Don't be unprofessional about any teacher you have seen or worked with whom you felt 'did not do it right': those reading it are likely to think this a little presumptuous.
- Ensure someone else reads your statement before you send it off. This provides a useful check to ensure you have actually written all that you wanted to write.
- Don't be afraid to offer some gentle humour or something that will make your statement stand out. If you have an interesting or slightly off-beat application form at interview this can mean, whether you are interviewed in a group or individually, the tutors will remember your application form and it could start an interview in a favourable way. However, do be careful, as if you go too far it may prove highly counter-productive.

The interview

The dress code here is smart but not casual. Teachers are respected members of society regardless of what you might read in the press and it is expected that you will dress in a way that promotes this professionalism. Teachers are not lawyers, so unless told otherwise wearing a suit is not expected, but male applicants should think seriously about investing in a tie and female applicants should consider something suitable for an interview and not a night out on the town! Jeans, regardless of their colour or their price tag, are generally not suited to a formal interview situation.

Ask the admissions department at your chosen institution about the format of the interview. There will often be some written task to assess your ability to write, punctuate and use attention-grabbing language, without the help of spellcheck on a computer. There will also often be a simple maths test to judge your numeracy skills.

There will be either a group interview and/or an individual interview. Don't assume all courses at the same university will do things the same way, as diverse requirements can often be found at the same institution on different programmes. The presentation or the group interview will assess your ability to communicate with others and your understanding of some issues. If a group task is used this is not to see who can take over and dominate the group, but to assess an applicant's ability to listen to others and work in a team. A good way to prepare for any teaching interview is to read up about current news items and *The Times Educational Supplement* is a great place to start. As stated in Chapter 2, this also has an on-line web forum, where prospective PGCE students can share experiences and discuss the types of questions, as well as offer advice on what to wear.

A key point to remember is that the interview process is two way; you have to like the institution and feel confident that you will enjoy learning there and that the course is right for you. So before applying, research the course, and the institution and attend any open day events to ensure when you do start a PGCE it will be the right PGCE for you.

Glossary

Advanced Skills Teacher (AST)
A teacher in a school in England who is assessed as having particular skills in a certain area. Part of that teacher's time is used in teaching a class and part in sharing skills with others.

Cross-curricular
Applying skills and knowledge from different disciplines to a single experience or theme.

Foundation and core subjects
In the current National Curriculum in England the subjects are divided into core and foundation, with the most often taught called core subjects (including English and mathematics) and the others foundation.

GTC
General Teaching Council – a body that leads and regulates the teaching profession, there is one for each country of the UK, so you will see the initials GTCE, GTCNI, GTCS and GTCW.

GTTR
Graduate Teacher Training Registry – a body that co-ordinates some applications for ITE from graduates. For some PGCE courses you must apply directly to the provider. There is also a GTTR for Scotland.

ICT/ ICT suite
Information Communications Technology – this includes working with computers. An ICT suite is a shared space in a school with enough computers for a whole class to use.

Induction
Usually the first year spent as a teacher after qualification.

ISA
Independent Safeguarding Authority – registers those who work with children.

ITE/ITT	Initial Teacher Education/Initial Teacher Training – these initials are sometimes used interchangeably but some people prefer to use ITE as it suggests a development of understanding as well as skills.
IWB	Interactive White Board – a large interactive display that connects with a computer and data projector.
LA	Local Authority – a county or unitary authority with responsibility for overseeing education and schools in the area.
Maintained school	A school that receives public funding.
Medium term plans/ unit plans	These plans are for work in an area of learning or subject that goes across several days, weeks or a whole term.
Mentor	An experienced teacher who has received some training in order to support student or new teachers in their professional development.
MTL	Master's in Teaching and Learning, a new qualification designed to enable teaching to become an all Master's profession. It is being gradually introduced in England and eventually all NQTs may be required to do it.
National Strategies	A term used in England to describe the National Literacy Strategy, the National Numeracy Strategy and the Primary National Strategy that these evolved into.
NQT	Newly Qualified Teacher – a teacher undergoing induction to the profession, sometimes called a Probationer Teacher in Scotland.
Nursery Nurse (NN)	A qualified professional who works with young children to support their wellbeing and assist in their education.
Ofsted	Office for Standards in Education – the inspection agency for schools in England. Wales has a similar agency – Estyn.

Partnership	In this book this word is used to describe an arrangement between a PGCE provider and local schools to enable professional development for student teachers.
Pedagogy	The principles and practice of teaching, sometimes referred to as the science and art of teaching.
PGCE/PDGE	Postgraduate Certificate of Education or Professional Graduate Certificate of Education awards given to student teachers as they complete their ITE. Postgraduate Diploma of Education is the equivalent award in Scotland.
Placement	A placement is a period of time spent in a school or other educational establishment during the PGCE course.
PPA	Planning, Preparation and Assessment – teachers will frequently have some non-contact time during a teaching timetable to enable them to carry out these tasks; they often call this PPA time.
QTS	Qualified Teacher Status – in order to become a qualified teacher you will need to meet certain criteria or standards, and when you are assessed as having met them you can be recommended to the GTC for QTS.
School policies	Each school is required to have a set of policies; these will include policies for teaching different subjects, behaviour, health and safety, etc. These guide the way these issues are approached in that school.
TA/LSA/LSW/HLTA	Teaching Assistant, Learning Support Assistant, Learning Support Worker – these are various titles given to school employees who work in a support capacity with children. A Higher Level Teaching Assistant will be a more senior employee who has usually received more training for the role.
Teaching pool	A pool of teachers, maintained by an LA, for schools in their area to call on when they have a vacancy.

Useful websites

www.tda.gov.uk	This is the Training and Development Agency for schools. It has information particularly for those working in England. This includes the Professional Standards for Teachers.
http://www.gttr.ac.uk	This is the Graduate Teacher Training Registry, through which you must apply for most PGCEs.
www.gtce.org.uk www.gtcw.org.uk www.gtcs.org.uk www.gtcni.org.uk	These are the addresses of the GTC websites for the four countries of the UK; they provide help and guidance, particularly on Induction into the profession when you are qualified.
www.ofsted.gov.uk www.estyn.gov.uk	As well as school reports, Ofsted (England) and Estyn (Wales) publish reports on subjects and issues in education.
www.dcsf.gov.uk www.scotland.gov.uk www.deni.gov.uk http://wales.gov.uk/topics/educationandskills	Each of the four countries has a government website or a section of their website devoted to education.
www.ttrb.ac.uk	Access to the research and evidence base informing teacher education.

www.tlrp.org	Teaching and Learning Research Programme – this organisation supports research to promote effective teaching and learning in the UK.
www.teachernet.gov.uk	A useful source of support, including information that can be downloaded and publications that can be ordered.
www.teachers.tv	Teachers TV has many programmes on a huge range of different topics that can help you learn and observe classroom practice.
www.behaviour4learning.ac.uk	An excellent source of theory and advice on promoting positive behaviour in the classroom.
http://www.multiverse.ac.uk/	This site provides resources and helps you to address the needs of pupils from diverse backgrounds.
www.nasuwt.org.uk http://www.teachers.org.uk/ http://www.atl.org.uk/	Websites for the teacher unions – you will want to be a member of one of these for support, insurance cover and advice.

References

Claxton, G. (2009) 'The Langton Lecture – What's the point of school?', 30 June.

Dewey, J. (1933) *How We Think: A Re-statement of the Relation of Reflective Thinking to the Educative Process*. Chicago, IL: Henry Regnery.

The Elton Report (1989) *Discipline in Schools: Report of the Committee of Enquiry*. London: HMSO.

Fuller, F.F. and Bown, O.H. (1975) *Becoming a Teacher*. Chicago: University of Chicago Press.

Griffiths, M. and Tann, S. (1992) 'Using reflective practice to link personal and public theories', *Journal of Education for Teaching,* 18(1): 69–84.

Kolb, D.A. (1984) *Experimental Learning*. Englewood Cliffs, NJ: Prentice Hall.

Moore, A. (2004) *The Good Teacher*. London: Routledge.

OFSTED (2008) *Grade Criteria for the Inspection of Initial Teacher Education 2008–11*. London: HMSO.

Pollard, A. (2002) *Readings for Reflective Teaching*. London: Continuum.

Pollard, A. (2008) *Reflective Teaching*. London: Continuum.

Schön, D. (1983) *The Reflective Practitioner*. New York: Basic Books.

Index

Academic writing
  appendices 48, 51–2
  bibliography 49
  case studies 47, 48, 54
  content 48
  criticism 54
  evidence, sources of 55–6
  formatting 48
  journal articles 57–8
  language 48, 52–4
  primary sources 56, 59
  quotations 50
  reading and development of ideas 46
  referencing: 48–9
  secondary sources 56, 59
  structure 48
  suggestions (for being academic) 59
Advanced Skills Teacher (AST) 35

Criminal Records Bureau (CRB) 23
  Primary PGCE 1–8

Finding work
  interview case study 97
  interviews 94–8
  interviews (key points) 95–6
  local authority pool system 86
  personal statement case studies 87–92
  personal statement review 93
  personal statement 86–92

General Teaching Council (GTC) 33, 99, 109
Graduate Training Programme (GTP) 5–6

Information Communication Technology (ICT)
    16, 25, 88–9, 92–3
Independent Safeguarding Authority (ISA) 23
Induction
  Newly Qualified Teacher (NQT) status 99
  work-life balance 100
  preparation 100–101

Induction *cont.*
  support and guidance 103
  induction tutor 103
  probation supporter 103
  lesson observations 104–105
  non-teaching commitments 105
  parents 105–106
  profession al development 107–109
  support 109–110

Mathematics 16, 37, 40, 91

Newly Qualified Teachers (NQTs) 99, 110
Nursery Nurse (NN) 28, 105

Ofsted reports
  commentary good or outstanding teachers 73
  research for PGCE courses 16
  research prior to placement 21

Positivity
  behaviour management 26
  mental attitude and success in PGCE 60–70
  working relationships 28
Primary PGCE
  courses available 5
  QTS 4, 5, 6
  suitability for 2–5
  why choose a PGCE? 6
PGCE assessment
  assignments 5
  oral presentations 5
  poster presentations 5
  placements 5
  theory vs. practice 6, 44, 45
  PGCE vs. GTP vs. SCITT
PGCE preparation
  behavior management 26
  attitude (being positive) 60–8
  case studies 14,17
  child assessment 29, 40–2

PGCE preparation *cont.*
  collaborative teaching 36–8
  criminal record bureau checks 18
  dress code 22
  health and safety rules 24
  internet forums 16
  learning through observation 13–14, 34, 35
  national curriculum 16
  needs analysis 16
  philosophy 10
  positivity (attitude, behavior, values) 60–70
  pre-course reading 16
  preparing lessons 28, 39, 40
  professionalism 33–4
  reading journal 16
  research 15–17
  self-assessment 30
  strategies 11–12
  time management 26
  university visits 16
Professional Graduate Certificate in Education
  courses
  full time 5
  part-time 5
  modular 5
Professional Graduate Diploma in Education
  (PGDE) 5

Qualified Teacher Status (QTS) 5–6, 16–17, 69,
  70, 72, 75, 87, 102

Reflection
  case studies 80, 81
  defining reflection 74
  development skills and development 76
  Donald Schon (reflection in teaching) 74

Reflection *cont.*
  informal/formal reflection 73
  Kolb's experiential learning cycle 74
  media 83, 84
  metacognition 77
  Ofsted comments upon 73
  practice examples 78–9
  QTS standards 73, 75
  reflection-in-action 75
  reflective discourse 75
  reflective events 75
  reflective journal or diary 77, 83
  reflexive reflection 77, 82

School Centred Initial Teacher Training
  (SCITT) 5, 6
Secondary sources 56, 59
Skills
  additional teaching skills 21
  child assessment 29
  English, mathematics, ICT requirements
    for QTS 16
  speaking and listening 91
  teaching development 43, 76
  transfer to classroom 5, 7
Special Educational Needs Co-ordinator
  (SENCO) 24
Social Networks ('nings') 16

Teaching Assistant (TA) 22, 28, 105
Times Educational Supplement (TES) 16
Transferable skills and attributes
  5, 7, 16
Teaching theory vs. practice 45, 46

Working with children 4

Reflective Practice
Writing and Professional Development · *Third Edition*

Gillie Bolton, *Freelance Consultant*

'A student of mine said that this book not only made him understand how to use reflective method with international perspectives, but opened up his postgraduate studies in many positive directions. I can think of no higher praise for a text that remains both core and contemporary and encourages professional creativity not only for teacher trainees and for students at Masters and Doctoral levels in Education but across many other subject areas' - *Richard Race, Senior Lecturer, Roehampton University, UK*

In the new third edition of this popular and highly readable book, the author draws on her considerable experience and extensive research to demonstrate a creative dynamic mode of reflection and reflexivity. Using expressive and explorative writing combined with in-depth group work/mentoring alongside appropriate focussed research, it enables critical yet sensitive examinations of practice.

New to this edition are:

- a new chapter presenting different ways of undertaking and facilitating reflective practice
- further international coverage, including material from Australia, New Zealand and USA.

Contents
Foreword / Acknowledgements / Mind the Gap: How to use this book / PART ONE: REFLECTION AND REFLEXIVITY: WHAT AND WHY / Reflective Practice: An Introduction / Reflection & Reflexivity / Principles of Reflective Practice / Through the Mirror / Writing as Reflection / PART TWO: REFLECTION AND REFLEXIVITY: HOW / Reflective Writing: a How-To Guide / The Learning Journal / Assessment and Evaluation / Group Processes and Facilitation / Reflective Practice and Team Development / Reflective Practice: Other Methods / PART THREE: REFLECTIVE WRITING: FOUNDATIONS / The Power of Narrative / The Power of Metaphor / Wider and Deeper: Other Writing Forms / Reflection on Reflection / Bibliography / Indexes

February 2010 · 304 pages
Paperback: 978-1-84860-212-0
Hardback: 978-1-84860-211-3

Find out more and order online at
www.sagepub.co.uk

Reflective Practice in the Early Years

Edited by **Michael Reed** and **Natalie Canning**

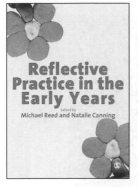

'This well edited book illustrates the importance of reflective practice in the early years through consideration of many contemporary issues and will be of interest to Childhood Studies and EYPS students as well as, practitioners and University tutors. The inclusion of many practical examples enables readers to make links between theory and practice, to examine their own practice and emphasises the powerful learning undertaken through considered reflection' - *Sue Kay-Flowers, Senior Lecturer, Liverpool Hope University*

Written for anyone working in the field of early years education and care, this book encourages students and practitioners to consider their own practice and to examine practice in a wide range of early years settings. The four sections link closely to the principles of the Early Years Foundation Stage, and support the reader in developing a critical and reflective approach to their own work.

Contents

Michael Reed and Natalie Canning Introduction / PART ONE: CHILDREN'S LEARNING AND DEVELOPMENT / **Karen Appleby** Reflective Thinking; Reflective Practice / **Natalie Canning** Play in the Early Years Foundation Stage / **Linda Tyler** 21st Century Digital Technology and Children's Learning / **Michael Reed and Alison Morrell** Policy to Practice in Wales / PART TWO: THE UNIQUE CHILD / **Claire Majella Richards** Safeguarding Children: Every Child Matters so Everybody Matters! / **Mandy Andrews and Kate Fowler** A Healthy Child - Direction, Deficit or Diversity? / PART THREE: ENABLING PROFESSIONAL ENVIRONMENTS / **Michael Reed** Children's Centres and Children's Services? / **Rosie Walker** Working together at a Children's Centre / **Wendy Messenger** Managing Multi Agency Working / PART FOUR: POSITIVE RELATIONSHIPS IN A MULTI-AGENCY WORLD / **Victoria Cooper** Distance Learning and Professional Development / **Rory McDowall Clark and Sue Baylis** Early Years Professionals: Leading for Change / **Alison Jackson** Defining and Measuring Quality in Early Years Settings / **Sue Callan** From Experienced Practitioner to Reflective Professional / **Michael Reed and Natalie Canning** Conclusion / **Michael Reed and Natalie Canning** Useful Websites

2009 · 232 pages
Paperback: 978-1-84860-162-8
Hardback: 978-1-84860-161-1

Find out more and order online at
www.sagepub.co.uk

SAGE Study Skills
Bestselling Guides for Students at all Levels

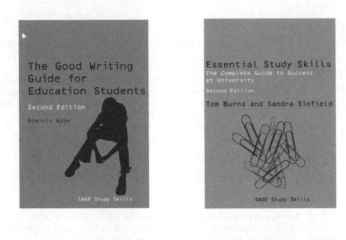

www.uk.sagepub.com/studyskills.sp